SIMPLY BUILD GREEN

A Technical Guide to the Ecological Houses at the
FINDHORN FOUNDATION

John Talbott

new, revised, expanded edition
May 1997

British Library Cataloguing-in-Publication Data.
A catalogue record for this book is available from the British Library.

Photographs by the author and Findhorn FoundationVisual Arts.
Original book design & reproduction by Posthouse Printing, Findhorn.
Cover design and layout of this edition by Findhorn Press.
Printed and bound by Interprint Ltd., Malta

Published by
Findhorn Press

The Park, Findhorn,
Forres IV36 0TZ, Scotland.
+44 (0)1309 690582 / fax 690036
e-mail thierry@findhorn.org
http://www.mcn.org/findhorn/press/ *or*
http://www.gaia.org/findhornpress/

Table of Contents

Preface

by Jonathon Porritt

Jonathon Porritt

I'm delighted to see the Ecological Village taking shape at the Findhorn Foundation. The research and application being carried out is invaluable to the rest of the world and I am glad so many people are visiting and making use of this green building technology.

It is vital that a project of this nature is encouraged to expand and that the knowledge and experiences gained in the process be shared with others. The support from the building industry and other related industries must continue to enable important research and the development of new building techniques. As more and more people will be incorporating ecological features into their own house designs, it is essential that the Foundation's Ecological Village acts as a demonstration centre for others to see how well green housing works and how attractive it looks.

Simply Build Green is an essential guide for any organisation or individual working with green buildings. Professionals and amateurs alike will benefit from reading of the basic philosophy behind the green buildings and the practical experiences of the Foundation in applying this philosophy to building over the past five years. By sharing information and encouraging a wider use of green technology the possibility of a sustainable future comes closer for all of us.

We must continue — in all aspects of life — to combat global warming. By taking into account materials and manufacturing processes when both designing and building ecological housing, we can all better play our part in saving the world.

Keep up the good work,

Yours sincerely,

Jonathon Porritt

Acknowledgements

The Findhorn Foundation would like gratefully to acknowledge the help and support of the many hundreds of people who have contributed to the ecological village project and the buildings that are described in this manual. There are far too many to be able to name them all, but a few must be mentioned.

Our heartfelt thanks to Ekkehard Weisner and Michael Schimmelschmidt of Keystone Architects, the original architects for the project; for their concept development, technical research and wonderful German humour; to Simon Clark for his amazing energy and stamina; to the Constructive Individuals' team of designers and trainers for their inspiration and support; to Uwe Welteke of Isofloc, Ökologische Bautechnik, for his 'Breathing Wall' concept, and the technical expertise, humour and patience needed to explain it (in English) to a slightly dense audience before we finally understood it; to the jolly team from Isofloc who travelled from Germany to demonstrate the wet-blown cellulose insulation system for our first house, with particular thanks to Sabine Knoll for her continued support in helping us with translation of technical advice by phone and fax; to Hartwin Busch of Auro Organic Paints for his willingness and helpfulness in answering endless questions about ecological building and product toxicity; to Roger Leaver and Wendy Turnbull of Excel Industries Ltd for their initial help with our building warrant, as well as continued assistance over the past three years; to Andrew Yeats of Eco-Arc Practice, for his enthusiasm, inspiration and unending stream of detail drawings; and finally the openness and willingness of our Department of Housing and Technical Services at Moray District Council to work with our unusual and innovative designs.

A very special thanks also to the many builders, in the form of members, associates and guests of the Findhorn Foundation, who have volunteered their labour since the project's beginning in 1987 and before. Requiring a special mention are Courtenay Young for his initial efforts as project manager for Bag End which got us into lift-off mode; Patrick Nash for making sense of the figures and keeping us solvent; Roger Doudna for pioneering and holding the vision for the ecological village and for his personal efforts in successfully building the first 'whisky barrel' house when all those around him doubted; Ian Cook for being as perfect a first client as we could have wished for; and that hard core of builders who stayed after the building schools were over and demonstrated great patience, endurance and ingenuity that first year, as we all struggled to work out the many problems unforeseen in this new system of ecological building. Also our thanks to the dozens of trainees who brought their inspiration and enthusiasm to our building courses; to the group of 'Elves' who worked the early and late hours doing the preparation and finish-up work that made those courses flow smoothly. It was a privilege to work with you all.

The Foundation would also like to acknowledge the many companies that have participated in our sponsorship programme over the past three years. A complete list of our sponsors and their products is included in Appendix D.

This book was made possible in part by a grant from Scottish Homes, Thistle House, 91 Haymarket Terrace, Edinburgh EH12 5HE. Scottish Homes is a National Housing Development Agency whose aim is to improve the quality and variety of housing in Scotland, through work in partnership with the public and private sectors.

Section 1
INTRODUCTION

Who This Technical Guide is For:

This technical guide was originally envisioned primarily to accompany our building course on ecologically sound houses and for the novice or aspiring self-builder interested in a 'greener way'. It includes a combination of standard building techniques and methods, like those for foundations and framing, necessary to any good quality house, and the basic philosophy of ecological building and its application, as seen through our own experience.

Since beginning this project of describing our experience we have discovered a much greater interest than we had anticipated and have received many requests for information about our buildings and ecological work, both from professionals in the building trade and from DIY enthusiasts wanting to convert their lofts in an environmentally sound way.

As a result we have widened the scope of the manual to give more background in the hope that it will serve the wider audience of those wishing to know what it means to build sustainably for the future. Our process is one that can be replicated anywhere, adapted to the particular local conditions, and carried out by enthusiastic and dedicated professionals and amateurs alike. We have tried to keep our buildings as simple and easy to build as possible, for purely selfish reasons: so we could manage to build them with our largely volunteer team.

Fig 1.1   Building School —trainers, trainees and 'Elves'

In the attempt to find the middle ground between understanding basic building and the more subtle technical nuances of things like the 'breathing wall', we have not been able to go into great depth in all areas. For some our descriptions may be too technical; for others not sufficiently so. But we hope that everyone will at least be able to benefit from what we have learned and avoid the mistakes we have made. With the large amount of research and experimentation being done in the field of environmental building there is far too much information to include in this basic manual, and we provide a further reading list for those wishing to delve deeper into this exciting topic.

Fig 1.2
Entrance sign at the
Findhorn Bay Caravan Park

The Findhorn Foundation

The Findhorn Foundation is an international spiritual community with a membership of some 150, situated close to the village of Findhorn on the Moray coast in Northeast Scotland. It was founded in 1962 by Peter and Eileen Caddy and Dorothy Maclean, based on belief in God and in an underlying Spirit and intelligence within all life. There is no formal doctrine or creed, but there is a common understanding that an evolutionary expansion of consciousness is taking place in the world, creating a human culture that is based on love, cooperation, wholeness and respect for all life. The Foundation is a charitable trust, its purpose being as a centre for education and demonstration to encourage and work with this emerging consciousness. In addition a growing number of individuals and families in the local area are associated with the Foundation. With the related activities and businesses we have the beginnings of a village of some 300 people.

Fig 1.3 Community photograph at the 30th Birthday Celebration

The Findhorn Community has long held a strong environmental ethic based on the idea of cooperation and co-creation with nature. We were first widely known for our work in the gardens, where phenomenal results were achieved under adverse conditions.

This took place in a caravan park, an unlikely choice since caravans are, environmentally speaking, arguably the worst possible dwelling in which to attempt to live in harmony with Nature. But it has given us the opportunity for a dramatic transformation as, nearly thirty years later, we begin to extend these same founding principles to the built environment. Through our new buildings, integrated landscape and infrastructure we intend to create a model of a sustainable and ecologically sound village.

Fig 1.4
A typical community caravan

The concept of developing a sustainable lifestyle for humanity is now becoming widely accepted not just as a good idea, but as something that is essential for our own and the planet's survival. A 'sustainable lifestyle' implies that the impact of our living on the planet will not deplete or in the long term adversely affect the natural environment in which we find ourselves. In other words, the earth is maintained and replenished through our collective actions upon it, and can therefore continue to sustain us indefinitely.

A simple example is that of a managed forest, where the number of trees cut down is matched or exceeded by the number of trees planted. That way the forest will continue ad infinitum and the tree harvesting is sustainable. Cutting trees without replanting means the forest is depleted and eventually disappears — obviously an unsustainable practice but one that is occurring in many places even today.

Human activity around the planet is currently very much in the non-sustainable mode, in almost any area one could choose to focus on. Stopping the destruction perpetrated on the biosphere through our collective actions and moving to a sustainable existence is now one of the key issues of our times.

To do that we feel that a new working model is needed. It is our hope that through our modest experiment we will discover better and more fulfilling ways to live and work together in active relationship with the other life forms and the natural world around us. This includes the physical systems — developing ecologically sound practices and materials. But it also includes the social, community and collective experience; the economic and wealth creation/sharing systems; and finally the context of human life — how it fits into our planet's own evolution and development — so that we may better know our place.

Introduction to Ecological Building

When we began to ask 'What is ecological?' in terms of building, it became clear to us that it is a complicated question and the answers are not simple or straightforward. It evokes images and feelings like caring for the environment, being 'green', being responsible for our actions, recycling, not leaving a trail of waste behind us. But what does it mean when you have to make choices between different products in order actually to build something? There is a noticeable absence of available data that considers the question. As we began our own research into products, materials and systems that might meet our criteria of sustainability, we found that it often wasn't easy to define the parameters against which we could fairly measure things. Each aspect of a product's manufacture and use — where it comes from and the impact of its production, installation, use and eventual disposal — can have far-reaching implications that require much study.

Fig 1.5 'Cornerstone', Eileen Caddy's house

To illustrate the point, it is estimated that a typical home contains something like 11,000 different products. If we were to take ecological awareness to the limit, we would need to research each one thoroughly and this alone could take many years. Indeed many individuals and groups around the globe are doing just that and we are learning more each year. At the same time, in the specific context of our building programme at the Findhorn Foundation, we felt a need to act: to ask as many relevant questions as we could think of and then choose the option that seemed the best, knowing that we don't have all the answers yet.

Some of the obvious questions we asked were: What are the energy and transport requirements of the product? What is the impact of the manufacturing process on the environment? How 'natural' is the product? What is its stability over time? What is its impact on residents living in the dwelling? What are the alternatives and the relative costs of each?

We found that we learned a great deal in this process, with many successes and some mistakes. We had to compromise at times, but we did make a start that we hope will be of use to others and that can be built on and expanded. What follows is an in-depth look at what we have learned to date. It is by its nature incomplete. Hopefully those who use this manual will add to and refine the information in it. Meanwhile we do hope it will provide a sound and firm foundation for others to make a start, enabling builders of all levels of skill to create beautiful and healthy buildings that don't cost the Earth, in any sense.

Fig 1.6 Findhorn Bay Caravan Park

Ecological Building

Pre-World-War-II buildings were made on the whole with natural materials, mainly because that was all there was within the limits set by the simple existing technologies, transport difficulties and cost. An additional factor was the availability of relatively cheap labour, which made the choice of materials more a matter of quality than of speed of construction. But with the development of modern transport and an abundance of fossil fuel power after the war, these restrictions disappeared. Cheap energy gave a new freedom to the manufacturing process, while an increase in labour costs due to rising standards of living added the new criterion of speed of construction. The advance of chemical technology and the advent of plastics and other mass- produced man-made materials meant that a whole new type of construction emerged. These new products, most of which had never been seen on Earth before, were used to replace traditional materials like timber, brick and stone.

Fig 1.7
Factory

Now, over 40 years later, the number of synthetic substances and chemicals used in the building industry has grown from a few dozen to over 5,000. And the numbers are still increasing, with over a quarter of a million new compounds worldwide being invented each year. Without the long-term testing and understanding of how these materials operate in practice, no one can know the effect they will have on human beings or indeed on the rest of the natural world. Many will be beneficial but many may not be and will have effects that will be known only after decades of use.

Already, however, some understanding is emerging with evidence of the outgassing of unstable compounds which causes serious toxicity of indoor air; the adverse health effects of modern sealed, non-breathing buildings, which concentrate the toxins even further; stress from artificial electromagnetic fields; radon gas poisoning; and the effect of the many other household chemicals and substances that go to make up our clothes, cleaning products, paints, furniture, carpets and even cosmetics.

The potentially crippling reaction to the accumulated chemicals trapped in homes and offices has been recognised as a condition called 'sick building syndrome' (SBS). The symptoms of SBS do not fit the pattern of one particular illness and cannot be associated with a single cause, but are the result of a complex synergy among low level contaminants. New medical practitioners/professionals, known as clinical ecologists, have emerged to treat these patients. Symptoms include eye, nose and throat irritation, congestion, lethargy, respiratory difficulties, fatigue, irritability, headaches, dizziness and difficulty with concentration. In some extreme cases buildings have been temporarily abandoned or even demolished when toxins could not be traced or controlled. In most cases symptoms disappear when the person is removed from the cause, i.e. the building, although some materials, asbestos being the worst offender, have long-term and/or permanent negative effects.

Fig 1.8
Holistic Health Department,
'Meridian'

It is clear that we cannot continue randomly to manufacture new building and home products without looking fully at other considerations, including health and overall ecological concerns, in addition to cost and convenience. The Findhorn Foundation's main goal has been to try to consider not only the larger ecological and global impact but also human health concerns.

Although the ecological criteria are hard to come by at the moment, from the point of view of human health there has been a considerable amount of research and writing done to date, and more is going on all the time. Because we spend nearly 90% of our time indoors, half of that in our homes, the quality of indoor air is vitally important to our health. The Environmental Protection Agency (EPA) in the USA is so concerned with the deteriorating quality of indoor air in homes that it has called it 'the most significant environmental issue we have to face now and into the next decade'.

Exposure to toxic materials in the home can occur in several ways. We can ingest them in our food, off our hands or in our drinking water, and absorb them through our skin or by being splashed in the eyes. But where we receive our greatest exposure to toxic substances in building products is from air pollution. The EPA has identified five major causes of indoor air pollution:

1. Biogenic particles (mould and bacteria that grow under certain conditions)
2. Combustion products (from tobacco, gas appliances etc.)
3. Organic chemicals (like benzene and formaldehyde used in building materials)
4. Naturally occurring health hazards (like radon and lead)
5. Fibrous materials and airborne particles (asbestos, fibreglass and pollen)

Biogenic particles can be controlled by preventing the conditions in which they thrive. Mould and mildew like damp, moist or humid conditions and can often form on the cold surfaces of poorly insulated walls, the cold wall, ceiling or floor providing the condensing point for airborne moisture. Through proper detailing of insulation to avoid these cold spots and ensuring adequate ventilation to reduce humidity, most problems with fungal growth can be eliminated.

Danger from combustion products inside the house can also be minimised by avoiding the use of unvented gas appliances or providing good ventilation and/or extractor fans where they are used. By far the greatest danger in this category is cigarette smoke, so just don't smoke or allow anyone else to do so in your house! Our collective policy within the Foundation is to ban smoking from all public buildings. Sorry smokers, but there is always the great outdoors which will at least give you a nature experience at the same time.

The third category, organic compounds, is perhaps where the greatest opportunity for improvement lies in the building materials area and we will return to it shortly.

Naturally occurring health hazards can also usually be avoided in new buildings through careful design, as in the case of radon, which is covered in Section 5.22. Radon is one of the most serious health problems in many homes but it can be remedied. As for other natural health hazards, it pays to be somewhat familiar with which ones are prevalent in your particular area and how to avoid them.

The final category, fibrous materials and airborne particles that are a mixture of man-made materials and other naturally occurring particles, can be dealt with in new buildings firstly by avoiding their use, as in the case of asbestos, and then by good detailing to eliminate loose particle ingress, for example, mineral wool fibres with air barriers, etc. Substances like pollen are more difficult to control and, depending on the sensitivity of the residents, special filtering of fresh air might be required if the problem is severe.

This is only a cursory look at these categories and possible solutions. Many of the difficulties addressed are the result of older technology and techniques which have now

Fig 1.9 Kitchen at House No. 4

been abandoned. These problems have been largely solved through better building regulations or by a ban on the use of the substance involved, again as in the case of asbestos.

What still needs to be addressed lies largely in the third category. Volatile organic chemicals (VOCs), solvents, chlorocarbons, formaldehyde, phenol and many other chemicals are all fairly rampant and are present in a myriad of different building materials, paints, decorating products and furnishings. These various compounds are unstable and to a varying degree make their way into the air we breathe. Solvents in oil-based paints, for example, including substances like toluene and xylene, both classed as narcotic and severe irritants, and benzene, a recognised carcinogen, are given off relatively quickly in the first few weeks after application. On the other hand the formaldehyde found in most particle boards and compressed wood products can continue to 'outgas' over a period of years.

It is through the choice of so called non-toxic building products that the danger of VOCs and other synthetic chemicals can be avoided.

Formaldehyde is perhaps the most common of this category of pollutants and deserves a special mention. It is classed by the EPA as a potential human carcinogen, but it will make you sick years before it will cause cancer. Low levels of exposure to formaldehyde can cause dizziness, nausea, eye and respiratory irritation and more serious long-term effects if exposure continues. It is found in upholstery, furniture, some types of foam insulation, permanent press clothing, carpets, curtains, glues and adhesives, and moulded plastics, to name just a few. But the biggest problem in building materials is in the particle boards and plywoods. In the form of urea-formaldehyde resin it can constitute up to 10% of the average sheet of compressed wood board. There are alternatives which are discussed in Section 3.05.

As a rule of thumb we have tried to avoid using anything containing formaldehyde or synthetic chemicals. The other important source of these compounds is in painting and decorating, and we have been fortunate to have found organic paints and wood preservatives that serve as high quality and high performance alternatives. These are discussed in Section 3.10.

Fig 1.10   House No. 4

There are those who claim that the formaldehyde problem is overstated, and that the disagreement between countries over the maximum levels of formaldehyde permitted in indoor air is proof that there is not a sufficient scientific consensus to justify the strict controls that are imposed. But this argument comes largely from the timber products industry. There is no real disagreement that formaldehyde is extremely unpleasant and a serious irritant, and that our exposure to it should be at least minimised or at best completely eliminated.

It is possible to have a healthy and environmentally friendly home despite the obstacles presented by the dominance of chemicals and synthetics in modern building products. No doubt as the evidence continues to emerge in favour of the non-toxic, low-energy and low-environmental-impact approach it will become easier. Eventually it may even become the norm for all houses. We hope so.

Building Biology — Baubiologie

Building Biology, or Baubiologie, is the study of the holistic interaction between human beings and the built environment. It is a movement which started in Germany to develop the knowledge and understanding of how buildings and materials affect people and to implement a system of building that aims to create a healthy living environment. Interest has now grown and there are wide-ranging and ongoing research projects and studies throughout Europe and North America. It has served as the guiding model for our buildings, the wealth of information and experience far exceeding any other source we could find at the time.

Building Biology looks at the interior climate/environment of buildings and attempts to duplicate as closely as possible the conditions found in the natural environment. It is a holistic and comprehensive approach that tackles root causes of problems and not treatment of symptoms. It is really a philosophy of building which takes into account health, the natural environment and human needs for shelter. It likens the built environment to our 'third skin' which, like our own skin ('first skin') and our clothes ('second skin'), needs to function naturally and in harmony with our human organism. That means it needs to be able to breathe, to function as a regulator, protector and insulator, allowing evaporation, absorption and communication with our natural environment.

Fig 1.11
Community Centre
lounge

Apart from the indoor climate created by the use of materials, Building Biology also attempts to look at other factors that affect our health in buildings. These include the siting of buildings, avoiding what has been identified as 'geopathic stress', and awareness of artificial electromagnetic fields (EMFs) generated by electrical systems, appliances, televisions, computer visual display units, microwaves, radio waves and powerlines. These are more subtle and less well understood health-affecting conditions, but there is a growing body of scientific evidence that these unseen fields do affect us and that our buildings can contribute to the either beneficial or negative effects they produce.

The use of colour in interior spaces, protection from noise pollution and the use of natural lighting are also important and are included in the design process.

The following list is a sample of some of the main design principles that Building Biology works with, as outlined in their *Working Papers in Building Biology*.

- Houses located away from centres of industry and main traffic routes.
- Houses located in spaciously planned developments with ample 'green' areas.
- Use of non-toxic and untreated natural building materials.
- Use of wall, floor and ceiling materials that allow air diffusion.
- Use of building materials that are hygroscopic (can absorb and release water vapour) to help moderate indoor air humidity.
- Interior surface materials that allow air filtering and neutralisation of air pollutants (i.e. materials capable of 'sorption').
- Balancing heat storage (thermal mass) and thermal insulation levels to provide a comfortable interior living temperature.
- The use of radiant heating and the use of solar energy wherever possible.
- Adequate protection from noise and infrasound vibration.
- Maximum use of natural daylighting and colours in the interior.
- Minimising artificial electromagnetic fields while maintaining natural magnetic and electrical fields.
- Use of construction materials that do not contribute to environmental degradation or pollution in any aspect of extraction, manufacture, installation and use, and do not exploit limited or endangered natural resources.

Fig 1.12
Managed forest for
sustainable supply of timber

The full set of *Working Papers in Building Biology* (19 chapters) and the accompanying correspondence course is available from the Institute of Building Biology (see Appendix E for details). The Institute has developed an assessment of building materials which, though still embryonic, is the only attempt we could find to compare materials over a wide range of criteria, from energy and ecological impact to permeability, natural radiation and human health impact.

This is a field that is growing rapidly as we become more aware of the way buildings and materials affect us. Already, in places like Germany where this movement toward healthy building has advanced beyond the theoretical to the practical, there are networks of suppliers of ecologically and biologically sound building materials. There is a process through which products are approved and can be certified as meeting the criteria of Baubiologie. No doubt this will eventually spread to Britain and other countries as we pause to think what we are doing to ourselves and the natural world through the built environment.

Original Brief for the Foundation's Eco-Houses

The first housing cluster for ten dwelling units was to be built on a site called Bag End, in the northeast corner of the Foundation's property at The Park, Findhorn. Many people will wonder where the name Bag End came from. It has often been mis-printed as 'Bad End' by the various suppliers that have shipped materials to us! It comes from J. R. R. Tolkien's *The Hobbit* and *Lord of the Rings*, and is the home of Bilbo Baggins, the two books' principal character. In the story Bag End is a place of serene pastoral beauty, very peaceful and cosy, with the resident hobbits, small furry creatures, living close to and in harmony with nature, blending with, and in some cases actually living in, the old trees there.

Fig 1.13
Original Bag End site
in early 1970s

Our site in many ways resembled this picture, with caravans nestled in amongst trees and plants put in by the Community more than 20 years ago on the barren sand dunes of what was once a Royal Air Force training camp. By 1989 when we began planning for the project, some caravans were barely visible amongst the summer foliage.

We wanted to ensure that whatever was built on the site would fit into it harmoniously. Because the planting that had taken place over the years was around the caravans that had been there, the sites were quite well defined and there were many semi-mature trees surrounding them. Our preference would have been for more attached housing or clusters of units joined together but in order to do this we would have had to clear large sections of the site, causing a lot of destruction in the process. This didn't really feel appropriate and certainly would not have honoured the huge amount of landscape work that the people before us had done.

This then became a major design decision, since it meant that the new houses would be on the whole self-contained and detached. However, within that restraint we also wanted them to share as many amenities and features as possible, to avoid the unnecessary duplication and cost so prevalent in modern housing estates. The sharing of

Fig 1.14   One of the whisky barrel houses under construction

amenities such as laundry facilities, workshop space, gardens, lounges or meeting rooms is one of the very positive benefits of clustered housing.

Having experimented with some unusual building forms in the past few years, including a 12-sided dining room extension, a 5-sided performing arts centre and round whisky barrel houses, we also wanted something that was *simple* to build. Round and multi-sided buildings, interesting and inspiring as they are, do take a lot more skill, time and money to build than more traditional pitched-roof rectangular ones. Or that is what we assumed and, having just spent 16 months (instead of our anticipated 6 months) on the 10-metre-diameter Community Centre dining room, we wanted to try something we thought would be easier. With our labour force consisting of mainly unskilled and semi-skilled volunteers, it was doubly important to keep it simple. In the vernacular of the day this means appropriate to 'self-build'.

We wanted the houses to be absolutely state-of-the-art 'green', employing the best methods and materials throughout in terms of energy, the environment and health considerations. As part of our initial planning group we had a landscape architect who was very aware of the growing concern about the adverse health effects of many building materials, and it felt particularly relevant to our situation that this be given special emphasis. So 'the healthy house' became one of our main themes.

In terms of style we wanted to establish our own kind of vernacular architecture and set a language of common materials that could form a harmonious pattern without limiting individual expression. Within this language individual members building their houses would be able to be creative and be fully involved in the process of design.

VIEW FROM SOUTH

Fig 1.15 Outline sketch elevation of Bag End house

We chose Ekkehard Weisner and Keystone Architects as our architects. With our simple brief we started formulating our concept design and initial site plan, working with a group of community members wanting to build there. The process of outline design and planning consent took about six months and we received planning permission in August 1989. Detailed design of individual dwellings then began. From that point the people who

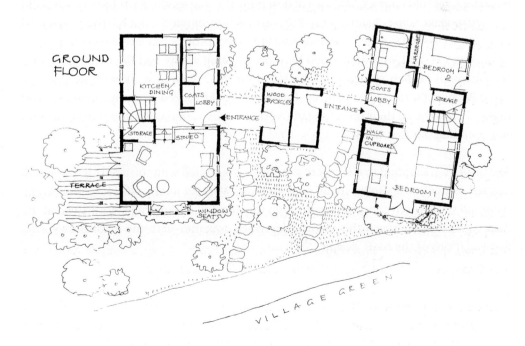

Fig 1.16 Outline sketch ground floor plan

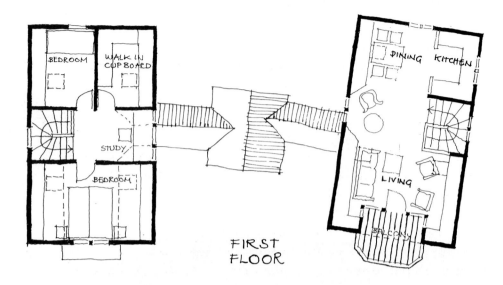

BEDROOM

WALK IN CUPBOARD

STUDY

BEDROOM

DINING   KITCHEN

LIVING

BALCONY

FIRST
FLOOR

Fig 1.17   Outline sketch first floor plan

would be financing their own houses began to work with an architect of their choice, drawing up their own brief and detailed design. Their final designs were then reviewed and approved by our in-house planning group before being submitted for planning permission to the local district council.

As the project developed we also came across a group called Constructive Individuals who run self-build courses. The idea of designing the houses along the lines of self-build seemed to make sense, again to keep the construction simple for our relatively unskilled builders. We visited Constructive Individuals' current project and saw one of their courses in progress, and were impressed by their teaching ability and the confidence that they inspired in their students. We arranged for their team to work with us and Keystone Architects, to ensure that our buildings would indeed be appropriate for self-build. We also hired their training staff to come to the Community and run a course to start building our first house.

The insulation standard that we were aiming for, combined with the need for easy building, led us to choose timber frame construction. Working jointly with Keystone Architects and Constructive Individuals through the detailed design stage, we arrived at the final construction, which this manual describes, together with the gradual evolution and variations of the basic design.

Principal Features

A condensed list of the principal features that we have researched and used in our houses follows. These are simplified descriptions and will be expanded in following sections.

- Use of passive solar features where possible through orientation and window layout.
- Use of solar panels for domestic hot water heating.
- A district heating system using a gas condensing boiler for highest fuel efficiency.
- High levels of insulation (U-values of 0.2 watts/m² C in roof, walls and floors).
- Use of low-energy light bulbs.
- Triple glazing (U=1.65 watts/m² C).
- Use of cellulose insulation (made from recycled paper).
- Non-toxic organic paints and wood preservatives throughout.
- Composite boarding manufactured without the use of toxic glues or resins.
- Locally grown and harvested timber from managed forests.
- Local stone for skirting, patios and pathways.
- Roofing with natural clay tiles.
- Innovative 'breathing wall' construction with a controlled exchange of air and vapour.
- Suspended timber floors for better air circulation to avoid a build-up of radon gas.
- Isolating electrical circuits to reduce electromagnetic field stress.
- Water conservation (showers, low-flush toilets and self-closing taps).
- Collection and recycling of rainwater for garden use.
- Shared facilities (laundry, kitchens, lounges) avoiding unnecessary duplication.
- Simple timber frame construction and detailing suitable for self-build.

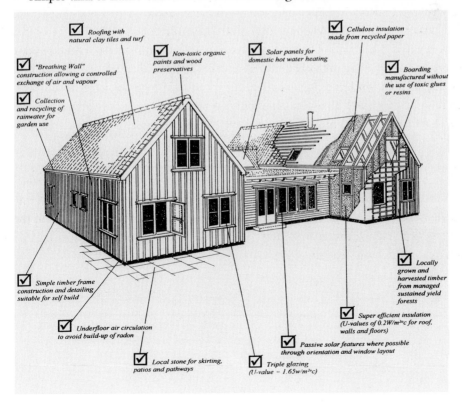

Fig 1.18 Cut away section showing features for shared 10-bedroom house

1.06 We have divided these features and other considerations we have taken into account into four main chapters:

2.00	Construction Types	4.00	Energy
3.00	Materials	5.00	Other Features

Each chapter may include a variety of specific topics and is generally detailed in two parts: 1) background and options, 2) our experience and findings. It is sometimes difficult to separate items into chapters, as many overlap, so these labels are somewhat arbitrary. It is intended that the last section of Section 5.10 on Services and Infrastructure will be expanded at a future date. In its present form it serves only as a very basic introduction to the subject.

Section 2
CONSTRUCTION TYPES

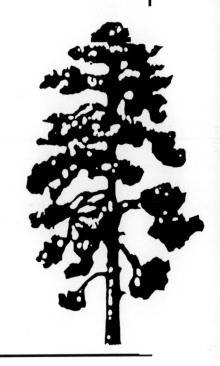

Introduction

There are many ways to build a house and before going too far you must decide which type of construction you will use. Walls, floors and roofs can all be of different types and one building can be a mixture of several different methods.

In Britain the earliest houses were simple structures of mud and straw with timbers supporting thatch, or stones piled into rough walls with sod roofs. They were crude and without much in the way of amenities but they performed the basic function of offering shelter from a harsh climate. We have come a long way from those early dwellings of several thousand years ago, and even from those of medieval times. In contrast to 'single skin' and largely uninsulated walls and roofs made from available local materials, we have developed sophisticated multilayered constructions that are full of exotic and highly processed components. Most modern construction methods are a vast improvement over our ancestors' building techniques, giving a much greater degree of comfort and protection. In the following sections some of the more common construction types used today are discussed, as well as our own choice. They are divided into components: foundations, floors, walls and roofs.

One of the chief criteria we used in selecting our construction type was the ease of building. Because of our requirement that semi-skilled people should be able to build the houses, timber construction won the day.

Fig 2.1 Framing of House No. 9/10

Foundations

Background

The main function of the foundations is to hold up the house, providing a firm and stable base over the natural soil which may have varying capacities to withstand loading. Foundations generally are intended to spread the weight, or load, of a building over a sufficient area of soil to avoid settlement, and especially unequal settlement which would lead to many problems in the building fabric. The transfer of the load is usually made to the horizontal surface of the soil but can also be made to the vertical surface as in the case of pile foundations. Foundations need to be able to support not only the weight of the building but also all the things that are likely to be in or on it, like furniture, fittings, people and snow.

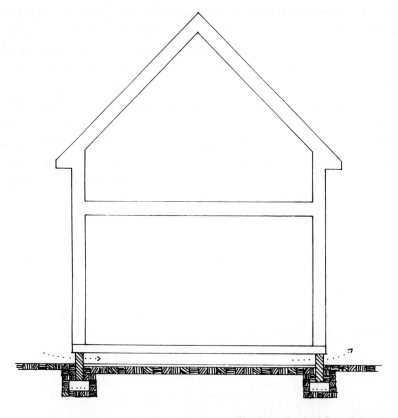

Fig 2.2   Typical foundation and house

Strip, wide strip, deep strip, pad, mass pier, raft and pile are all different kinds of house foundation. The particular one you choose will depend on the wall construction and how it needs to be supported, how the building itself is being supported, the ground conditions and, of course, the soil type and its bearing capacity. With the exception of pile foundations, concrete (a mixture of cement, sand and rock, or aggregate) is the universal material used for foundations. It is very strong in compression and ideal for transferring loads from walls or columns to the soil. However, it is weak in tension. Foundations that are subject to any bending movement, which involves a tensile stress, may need to be reinforced to give them extra strength. Steel is the normal reinforcing material and is very strong in tension. So steel-reinforced concrete foundations offer the best strength qualities of each material. Both concrete and steel come in different stress grades for different conditions. Pile foundations can be made from timber or steel as well as concrete. Foundation design and soils engineering are complex skills and should always be carried out by a qualified person.

Strip Foundations: Most small buildings of a residential nature have one of the varieties of strip foundation. A continuous strip of concrete evenly distributes the loads from the walls to the ground. It is placed centrally under the walls, located far enough below ground to avoid any ground movement from freezing weather, called frost heave, which could cause damage to the concrete and lead to settling of the building, as in the leaning tower of Pisa. The depth of the strip is determined by local regulations which will be based on the specific weather conditions for the area you are building in. The strip is always wider than the wall and serves to spread the load of the building over a larger area, thus reducing the pressure on the ground. If a much wider strip is needed to meet the soil-bearing capacity of the particular site it may need reinforcing across its width, and is surprisingly called a 'wide strip' foundation. Or, if the ground conditions dictate that a strip must be very deep, the excavated trench may simply be filled up with concrete instead of a thinner concrete strip with built-up block work, and is called a 'deep strip' foundation, amazingly enough. This makes the foundation easier to construct because it avoids laying blockwork in a deep hole, but it takes more concrete.

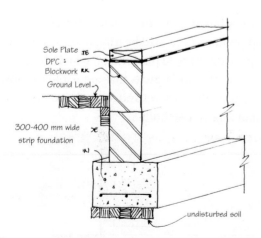

Fig 2.3
Section of strip foundation

Pad Foundations are similar to strips in that they spread the load horizontally on to the earth, but instead of supporting a continuous load-bearing wall they support a point load, usually a column or one edge of a beam. The thickness of the pad and whether or not it is reinforced are determined by how the load is applied and other particular conditions, but the thickness is usually never less than 150 mm.

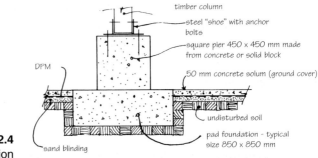

Fig 2.4
Section of pad foundation

Mass Pier Foundations are similar to pads but very much thicker, sometimes a metre or more deep. As well as transferring the load vertically to the horizontal surface of the ground below them, pier foundations give added resistance to fracture from unequal loading and usually won't require reinforcement.

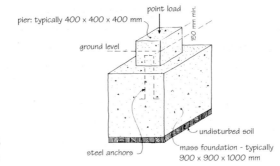

Fig 2.5
Section of mass pier foundation

A **Raft Foundation** is a cast slab that is poured over the whole floor area of the building and thickened at the walls and points where load-bearing occurs. It is reinforced throughout and acts like a 'raft', providing a rigid platform on which the house sits. It is best suited to areas of soft natural ground or areas that are liable to subsidence and it has the added advantage of providing a level and smooth working surface on which other elements of the building can be built.

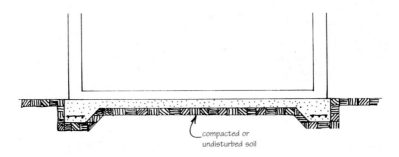

Fig 2.6 Raft foundation

Pier Foundations are usually used for larger buildings where the soil is unstable. They can either be 'end bearing' piles where the pile is deep enough to go through the unstable layers to solid ground or rock; or 'friction' piles where the soils are cohesive enough to provide resistance to vertical movement along the length of the pile from surface friction. Only in extreme conditions would piles be used in house construction, as they tend to be deep and expensive.

Our Experience

We have tried several different types of foundations. In the first two houses we used mass pier foundations located to support timber ground beams, which in turn supported the walls and floor joists. The idea was to leave the soil exposed under the house, to let it breathe, and thus literally 'live lightly' on the earth. But we found that the building regulations in Scotland require not only a damp-proof membrane (dpm) but also a minimum 50 mm concrete screed. There is no good reason for this, although the Building Control officers will argue differently, and it is a pity to have to cover the ground needlessly with concrete. The reasons they give are: to protect the underside of the house from moisture and dampness given off by the ground and to prevent plant growth. But given that the piers were to have been spaced quite widely (2.5 m) and the ground beams raised 300 mm above ground, giving very free air flow, moisture would certainly not have been a problem. As for plant growth, with many caravans on the site, none with dpms or concrete screeds, one need only look underneath any one of them to discover that plants don't grow in the dark!!!

We discovered this solum regulation only a few days before we were due to begin the first house. The point of not covering any more of the earth with concrete than was structurally necessary was lost. Digging deep holes for mass piers is not easy and getting the concrete into them without caving in the sides is extremely tricky and so, once we realised there was no way around the silly solum requirement, we abandoned the mass piers approach. Building timber ground beams is also a dubious operation, taking a lot of time and timber.

Fig 2.7
Picture of ground beams under construction, House No. 5

Because of the radon problem (see Section 5.22) we decided not to opt for a raft foundation, although it is perhaps the easiest and most convenient of the foundation types because of its shallow depth and the resulting flat, clean work surface that can be used during the construction process.

The next evolution was to the strip foundation. We were also experimenting with our structural system, how the loads were transferred through the building to the foundations. We used three strips, one at each outside wall and one in the centre to support the floor joists, with two courses of blockwork to take the level up to the sole plate and wall. We left the gable ends open for the maximum air flow under the building. We did not allow for any crawl space between the solum and the bottom of the joists, which we later regretted and have since changed. This was a much easier excavation process than the mass pier foundations and fairly easy to pour. Laying blockwork is a more skilled job and it meant that we then needed a good bricklayer.

This foundation was for a traditional 1½ storey house where the rafters are tied to the floor joists, forming a natural truss, which means the rafter 'thrust' from the angle of the roof is resisted so they need no other support. In order to create slightly more usable floor area in the first floor we raised the roof, and the rafters then needed to be supported internally to avoid the thrust force at the outer walls. (See the following Section 2.06 on structure.) This led us to use internal columns that needed support on pad foundations. We have combined the strip foundation for walls with pads for columns and have a kind of hybrid between load-bearing stud wall construction on the exterior walls and posts and beams in the interior.

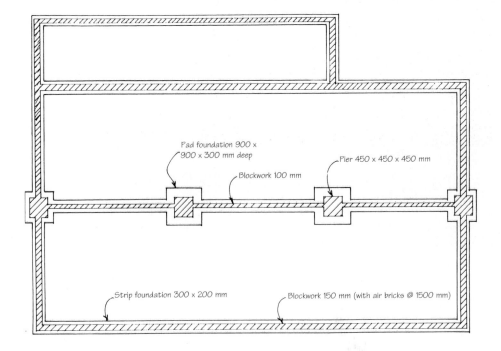

Pad foundation 900 x 900 x 300 mm deep

Pier 450 x 450 x 450 mm

Blockwork 100 mm

Strip foundation 300 x 200 mm

Blockwork 150 mm (with air bricks @ 1500 mm)

Fig 2.8   Foundation plan, House No. 4

We have also lowered the solum to below ground level to give us a crawl space without lifting the buildings higher off the ground. It means that the interior block surfaces must be coated with tanking material to prevent water building up in the solum space. We have enclosed the gable wall ends with blockwork to prevent little animals from entering but have provided ample air bricks to allow the air to circulate freely under the house.

Fig 2.9
Strip foundations

Floor Construction

We have two distinct floor types: internal floors, as in the first floor separating the upstairs and downstairs; and the ground floor, which separates the inside ground floor rooms from the underside of the house. Each type has its own specific design parameters.

Background — Ground Floor

The two types of structure for ground floors are concrete slab or suspended timber. Slabs can be poured either on top of a reinforced raft foundation or over the appropriate fill material between strip foundations. Suspended timber floors have floor joists running some distance above the solum supported at appropriate intervals by ground beams or small masonry (dwarf) walls on foundations. Concrete floors provide a hard surface for tiling or stone work and have good thermal mass, but can also be hard and uncomfortable to live with. They can be strapped with wooden battens and a conventional wood or other subflooring laid on top. Ground floors need to provide good protection against damp, be well insulated against the cold and prevent the build-up of radon gas.

Our Experience — Ground Floor

In our houses we have used suspended timber floors primarily because of our 'breathing wall' construction, discussed in Section 2.05, as well as for the ease of construction, avoidance of radon and extra thermal insulation this system provides. Joists are 50 x 150 mm or 50 x 200 mm, usually at 600 mm centres and supported by dwarf walls at one or two places between the side walls, depending on the span. 'Dwangs', short pieces of timber used for blocking between joists, or herringbone struts are used at the midpoints of the spans to give lateral stability to the joists, and the spaces between joists are infilled with cellulose insulation. In all the houses so far we have used 27 mm tongue-and-groove softwood flooring as the finished floor, with no subfloor. This has not been totally satisfactory because of the shrinkage of the wood, opening gaps in the joins, and in some cases cupping. See Section 3.09 on floor coverings.

To hold the loose insulation between the joists we needed a rigid board and we have used 12 mm bitumen-impregnated fibreboard, the same as we used on the walls. We have had some difficulties with it because we put it in before the building was watertight. When it rains water tends to collect on it and causes it to weaken and sag, and sometimes even collapse. We discovered the error of our ways in not providing a crawl space under the house when we had to try and repair several places after the floor had been laid. We have now realised that the building must be watertight before putting in the fibreboard, although we were on the seventh house before we finally figured this out.

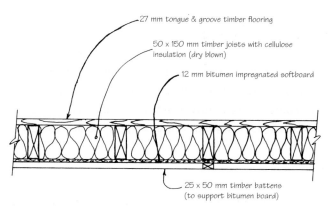

Fig 2.10
Section
of ground floor
construction

2.02

27 mm tongue & groove timber flooring

50 x 150 mm timber joists with cellulose insulation (dry blown)

12 mm bitumen impregnated softboard

25 x 50 mm timber battens
(to support bitumen board)

The ground floor can also be a major source of draughts and care needs to be taken to eliminate gaps around columns, walls and sole plates where air may be able to leak in. The cellulose insulation we use is excellent at filling these potential heat-losing areas but if a less air-resistant insulation material is used, like mineral wool, it is a good idea to incorporate an air barrier, like a breathable paper, under the sub-floor.

Background: Internal Floors

In residential construction involving relatively small buildings, the internal floor construction will be almost universally of timber, using an appropriate-size joist and spacing to carry the internal floor loads. Apart from the floor strength, another important property of an internal floor is its ability to provide good sound insulation. This is not always easy to achieve in a timber building with less mass to absorb sound.

In floor construction where timber joists are used for fixing the ceiling cladding and the flooring so that the joist spans the full depth of the floor, sound transmission is usually a problem. No amount of insulation between joists will help, as most of the sound is transmitted through the joists, which act like little amplifiers. So some special care needs to be taken if you want to have good sound-proofing. This may not always be the case, for example, in a small house where the residents are all one family and don't care so much about overhearing one another. But where houses are shared by different individuals and privacy is important, good detailing of the floor construction is essential. Thermal insulation is also standard procedure so that if rooms above or below are kept at different temperatures there won't be undue heat loss between them. Often thermal insulation will form part of the sound-proofing methods.

Our Experience

We have tried several methods but the most successful to date sound-wise was the one we used in our first two houses — the 'floating floor'. Joists are covered with a subfloor of 18 mm plywood (the only place we used plywood) followed by a 25 mm layer of fibrous quilt, a stiff matting made of coconut fibre; then a layer of 19 mm plasterboard, a special product with lapped edges for floor applications, giving extra density to absorb sound; and finally the 27 mm t & g softwood flooring. The timber floor is actually not nailed but 'floats' on the plasterboard and fibrous quilt. It is glued at the edges and forms one continuous surface over the whole of the first floor. The joists are infilled with cellulose insulation and the ceiling below is standard 12.5 mm plasterboard. We used plywood in this case for structural reasons, no other easy alternative being available. We have now replaced it with solid wood subfloor, which is possible in the context of the structural system we are using currently.

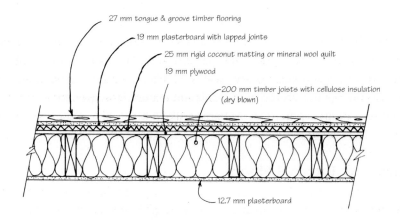

27 mm tongue & groove timber flooring

19 mm plasterboard with lapped joints

25 mm rigid coconut matting or mineral wool quilt

19 mm plywood

200 mm timber joists with cellulose insulation (dry blown)

12.7 mm plasterboard

Fig 2.11   Section of floating floor

In some of the other houses we tried to simplify the floor, using felt strips on top of the joists and other semi-homemade remedies to reduce sound. Basically they didn't work. A fairly easy way to improve sound-proofing is to use timber battens running perpendicular to the floor joists to either hang the plasterboard ceiling or lay the subfloor. This reduces the area where solid timber spans the floor depth, the place where most sound is transmitted. We plan to try this in our next house.

Wall Construction

Background

Solid Masonry: Not normally used in modern construction because of its generally low thermal insulation level, it was at one time the most common type of wall. Using either stone or brick, walls were built in thicknesses of up to a metre, depending on the height of the structure. Masonry is a poor insulator, as anyone knows who has lived in a building of Victorian vintage. These houses take a long time to warm up and do not hold the heat well. It is possible to use solid masonry walls and still meet the British Building Regulations for insulation by using lightweight blocks that have higher thermal resistance. But given that the British standards are far lower than we think they should be, as well as by other European standards, this is not an option for energy-efficient design. However, there are new 'insulated blocks' incorporating a foam inner core that can give a good level of insulation. They are still rare in Britain but are used extensively in Europe and especially Scandinavia.

Masonry Cavity Wall: Made from clay or concrete bricks or blocks, two independent walls are constructed and linked together with metal connectors or 'wall ties' inserted at regular intervals to give stability. Walls are usually 100-150 mm thick with the cavity between them 50-100 mm. In more energy-conscious buildings the cavity is filled with insulation material. It is possible to achieve high insulation standards with this type of construction by using thermal blocks with cavity wall insulation. Advantages of masonry walls are that they are good sound insulators, require little maintenance and are very good at protecting against the weather!

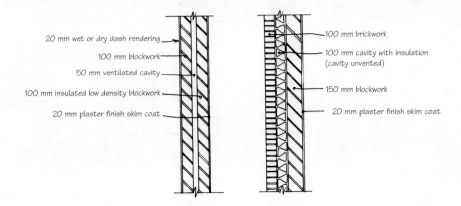

20 mm wet or dry dash rendering
100 mm blockwork
50 mm ventilated cavity
100 mm insulated low density blockwork
20 mm plaster finish skim coat

100 mm brickwork
100 mm cavity with insulation (cavity unvented)
150 mm blockwork
20 mm plaster finish skim coat

Fig 2.12   Wall sections of two variations of masonry cavity wall construction

Timber Frame Cavity Wall: Growing in popularity within the building industry because of ease of construction and high insulation level, this method consists of a timber stud inner wall and a masonry outer wall with a cavity in between. The tim-

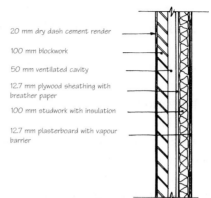

Fig 2.13
Section of timber frame
and masonry wall

20 mm dry dash cement render

100 mm blockwork

50 mm ventilated cavity

12.7 mm plywood sheathing with
breather paper

100 mm studwork with insulation

12.7 mm plasterboard with vapour
barrier

ber wall is sheathed on the cavity side with plywood and on the inside with plasterboard, and varies between 80 and 150 mm in thickness. The timber frame acts as the structural support and is put up first, with the masonry wall, normally made from either brick or concrete block, added after the building is watertight. The outer wall serves mainly as weather protection or cladding, adding little to the insulation of the house but providing a low-maintenance exterior surface. The advantage of this type of construction is that the inner structure can be put up and made watertight quickly, allowing the interior finishing work to start while the exterior masonry walls are still being built. The stud walls, with spacing of the studs usually at either 400 or 600 mm, provide a convenient place to put thermal insulation at a reasonable thickness.

Fig 2.14   Erection of wall, first Building School, House No. 5

Timber Frame — Timber Clad: Much more popular in Europe and North America than in Britain, this is a single wall construction using timber infilled with insulation and also using timber as the weather-protection layer instead of an additional wall of masonry. It is lightweight and easy to construct and provides the necessary space for insulation. The timber cladding does require regular maintenance to protect it. Two main types of timber construction are used: stud wall and post and beam.

Stud Wall: This is the most common method today because it uses small dimension timber, which is readily available. Vertical members, or studs, are placed at frequent intervals between two horizontal members, a 'head plate' at the top and 'sole plate' at the bottom. Stud walls are easy to build, and can be assembled flat on the ground and tipped up into place. Usual stud sizes vary from 40 to 50 mm wide and 80 to 200 mm deep, and can be adjusted to allow for whatever level of insulation is needed.

Post and Beam: The other main timber construction method is the post and beam, often referred to in North America as the timber frame. In Britain the term 'timber frame' is sometimes used erroneously for stud wall construction. Post and beam construction uses large dimension timber to support the smaller dimension members like joists and rafters. Beams over large spans and spacing are supported by columns or posts, which in turn transfer the load to the foundations. Walls are non-load-bearing, infilling between the posts. The posts and beams are generally made up on the ground in large frames and either tipped up into place (a 'barn raising' requiring lots of neighbours or a crane) or disassembled and then rebuilt in place. The advantage of post and beam is that the frames can be made on the ground then assembled very quickly. Once the roof is decked and felted the rest of the building can be built under

Fig 2.15   Post and beam frame of Community Centre extension

cover. Because the walls are not carrying the weight of the building there is much more freedom in choosing the materials, finishes and insulation and in locating windows and doors.

This is the method of construction of the traditional timber-framed English cottage, with blackened timbers left exposed on the outside and the panels often filled with exposed brick or wattle and daub, plastered with a white, lime-based render. Many different methods of timber-framing evolved between the early 13th and the late 18th century to make more efficient use of timber as forests became depleted and good building oak scarce.

There are of course many hundreds of other wall construction methods and this list includes but a select few of the more common types in Britain.

Our Experience

Because of our desire to use a renewable source of material for as much of the building as possible, as well as our concern about suitability for self-build, we chose timber for the framing and cladding. All the exterior walls are studwork, using 50 x 150 mm softwood, mixed spruce, fir and pine from our local mill. The exterior of the studwork is sheathed with bitumen fibreboard, the inside with 9 mm medium board and 12.5mm plasterboard. Because of our 'breathing wall' construction we require two inner boards instead of the normal single plasterboard layer. To give enough air flow over the exterior wall surface, vertical counterbattens and horizontal battens are used to give a 50 mm cavity under the timber cladding. All battens and cladding are fixed with galvanised lost head nails.

Fig 2.16
Timber board
and batt cladding

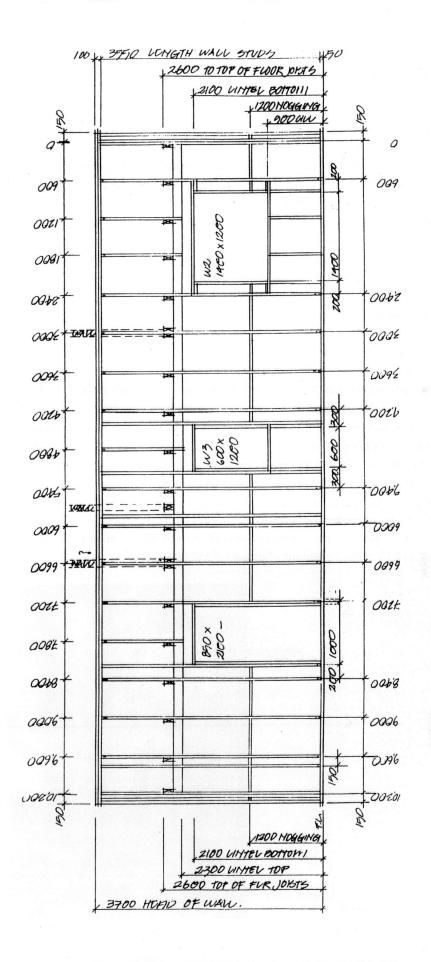

Fig 2.17 Typical wall framing drawing

Roof Construction

Background

Although there are other materials that roof structures can be made from, such as metal and concrete, for the scale of building in residential houses timber seems the only real choice. The two main methods for pitched roof construction using timber are trussed rafter or plain rafter. There are many variations possible in both methods. The main advantage of the trussed rafter is that it can be designed and built to minimum tolerances by specialist companies and delivered on site ready for erection. It is by far the most common roof structure used today. The main disadvantage is that the bottom chord of the truss reduces the ceiling height of the room by limiting it to being flat. In other words it is difficult to have a finished ceiling that is vaulted. Although trussed rafters can be adapted to accommodate better use of the loft space, this is usually not the case and they are not as flexible as plain rafters.

With plain rafters each one is cut to fit on site and is generally made larger than required to account for differences and defects in each particular one. The advantage of plain rafter framing is that there are many variations on how the rafters can be supported, giving a lot more freedom to be creative with the ceiling — vaulting it, creating more usable space, like lofts, etc. This kind of roof structure is more time-consuming to erect but it can give more life and interest to the interior spaces.

Insulation can be applied either on top of the roof deck, between the rafters, or in the flat loft area between the bottom chords of trussed rafters. In either case care has to be taken to avoid a build-up of moist air and condensation.

Fig 2.18
Vaulted roof in
House No. 7 living room

Our Experience

We chose plain rafter framing for both aesthetic and design reasons as well as for the fact that most truss companies will not sell trusses made with untreated wood. We have used several different methods for supporting the rafters but have generally left the roof space completely open to the first floor rooms, providing roof lights, high level gable end windows and dormers to bring natural light into the upper areas. The effect is quite stunning and creates a much larger and more interesting living space. This would not be possible with trussed rafters.

The rafters are boxed in using the same construction as the walls and infilled with dry blown cellulose, the exception being in the roof sarking which is bitumen-impregnated fibreboard — more durable than the wall board— with special profiled edges for shedding water. A roofing felt is placed between the counterbattens and tiling battens and the roof is covered with interlocking clay pantiles.

We chose clay tiles because of the natural properties of clay, their competitive cost and the ease of installation. The alternatives we considered were:

Slate: expensive and requiring a skilled tradesperson.
Concrete tiles: not a particularly ecological choice, though inexpensive and fairly easy to install.
Cedar shakes: a natural material but available only from North America where it is being harvested unsustainably and is required by Building Regulations to be heavily treated with preservatives.
Asphalt shingles: cheap and easy but non-breathable, requiring a more complicated roof construction for our 'breathing' buildings and not a particularly ecological material.

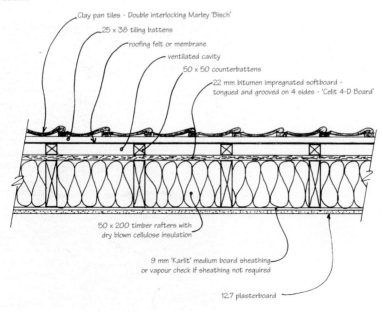

Clay pan tiles - Double interlocking Marley 'Bisch'
25 x 38 tiling battens
roofing felt or membrane
ventilated cavity
50 x 50 counterbattens
22 mm bitumen impregnated softboard - tongued and grooved on 4 sides - 'Celit 4-D Board'
50 x 200 timber rafters with dry blown cellulose insulation
9 mm 'Karlit' medium board sheathing or vapour check if sheathing not required
12.7 plasterboard

Fig 2.19   Section of roof construction

Our experience with clay tiles is discussed more fully in Section 3.03, but overall we have been satisfied with them.

Flashing for the valleys, dormers and rooflights would normally be done in lead. We were keen to use our rainwater runoff from the roof for watering gardens and were advised against lead because of the possible contamination and a resulting build-up of lead in the soil. Just what effect the lead would have has been difficult to verify but to be safe we decided to avoid using it as much as possible. Instead we used copper and, in a few places, glass-reinforced plastic. Where we couldn't avoid using lead was around rooflights, which come as a kit with a small lead apron around the base of the unit. While lead is malleable and forgiving, copper is not and needs the skill of an experienced roofer to install properly.

The 'Breathing Wall'

Background

In line with keeping the interior environment as pollution-free and healthy as possible, we have tried to follow the principles of Building Biology in our wall, roof and floor construction. Indoor air quality is most affected by pollutants given off by building materials and those generated within the house. It is what we, as occupants, breathe directly and, as we can spend something like 90% of our time inside buildings, it is worth the effort to keep the air quality high. Going back to basic Building Biology principles, we are reminded that we should select materials to allow for maximum air diffusion, using those that have high hygroscopicity and that can filter and neutralise possible pollutants. In other words they should be able to 'breathe', with a certain amount of exchange of air, water vapour and particles. This will improve the quality of the indoor air and reduce the fresh air requirement within a house, minimising unnecessary heat loss.

In pre-1920s' construction, houses generally were made from materials that could breathe, such as brick, gypsum plaster, lime plaster, clay and timber. Windows and doors were not tightly sealed and ventilation through draughts was extensive, avoiding any moisture build-up in indoor air. The absence of chemicals and the high ventilation rates kept the inside air quality high. Of course, these buildings tended to be badly insulated and were generally cold (or used larger amounts of energy to heat), which led to other health-related problems for occupants. But essentially these buildings did meet the 'breathing' criteria, albeit in a fairly inefficient and random way.

With energy conservation and modern materials the situation has been reversed. Buildings are more tightly sealed, which reduces the indoor air quality, but they are also easier to heat and keep warm. Essentially these modern buildings have become more energy-efficient but in the process they have stopped breathing, which results in what one could call 'dead' air space inside. In many ways it is actually true that the 'living' and breathing qualities of materials used in buildings has been largely ignored or considered unimportant. The key factors instead have become cost and ease of construction.

We developed the modern version of the 'breathing house' by going back to many of the traditional materials listed above but adding good insulation levels and more and/or better control of air ventilation rates. We dubbed the particular construction we developed 'the breathing wall' because it does take into account and use the natural properties of materials in terms of permeability and diffusion and, through careful selection of materials, allow controlled exchange of air and moisture.

To understand the problem and its solution better, some discussion of the basic principles and behaviour of insulated building fabric is needed. A principal concern of building scientists in highly insulated buildings is 'interstitial condensation'. This is when water vapour condenses within the wall structure and is allowed to build up, leading to bacterial and/or fungal growth and resultant damage to the building structure as well as unhealthy living conditions inside. Moisture-laden warm air from within the house (generated by cooking, baths and showers, and people themselves) tends to travel through wall and roof sections, driven by the need for equilibrium with the outside air which is colder and drier. The temperature of the air gradually drops as it passes through the insulation and may eventually reach the 'dew point', i.e. the temperature at which no more water vapour can be held in the air. At this point the same phenomenon occurs which we witness outdoors in the cool evening or early morning air when suddenly everything becomes damp with dew, and grass and leaves glisten with water droplets.

Warm air has a greater capacity to hold water vapour than cold air does and as the air cools, the saturation point is reached when the water *vapour* condenses to form *liquid* water. For example, if indoor air is at 20°C and 70% relative humidity (RH), as it passes through an insulated wall water will condense when the temperature reaches 14°C. If the outside air is at 1°C and 40% RH, the inside air will have lost over 90% of its water by the time it reaches the outside surface of the wall. In other words the inside air of this example can hold 10 times the amount of water vapour by weight than can the outside air.

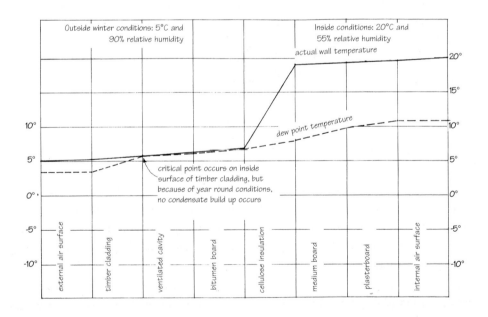

Fig 2.20   Temperature profile — Breathing Wall construction

Water build-up inside a wall will reduce the effectiveness of insulation and lead to quite serious problems like wet rot and dry rot of wood and the decay and structural breakdown of materials. These have serious consequences for both health and safety. In extreme cases buildings have been known literally to fall down from the effects of condensation. So the construction of a wall does need to be carefully designed to avoid these problems.

The modern solution to interstitial condensation has been to seal the fabric against the ingress of water vapour, usually by incorporating a 'vapour barrier' in the wall and construction and providing ventilation on the outer surface of insulation. This is usually in the form of polythene (plastic) sheeting or aluminium foil. Plasterboard with foil bonded to the back is often used or, alternatively, mineral wool insulation mats with foil-faced paper. Vapour barriers are always placed near the *inside* wall surface as one of the first layers, to stop the vapour travelling through the wall at source.

Of course, this solution also eliminates any *beneficial* air and moisture exchange that could take place between inside air and materials within the wall, and the tight seal of modern windows and doors often means that the house may need mechanical ventilation to get enough fresh air. Recent studies have shown that having to rely on mechanical ventilation can lead to problems, both in terms of reliability of the system and because of the build-up of health-damaging bacteria and micro-organisms in the air ductwork.

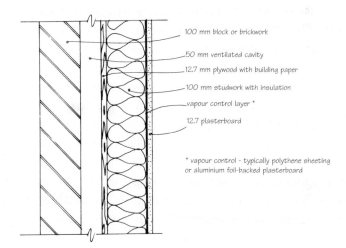

100 mm block or brickwork

50 mm ventilated cavity

12.7 mm plywood with building paper

100 mm studwork with insulation

vapour control layer *

12.7 plasterboard

* vapour control - typically polythene sheeting or aluminium foil-backed plasterboard

Fig 2.21
Section
of typical wall
construction

Vapour barriers are not the only method of avoiding condensation in the building fabric. BS 5250 is the British Standard that deals with the avoidance of interstitial condensation and provides a method of determining by calculation whether a wall will have condensation problems under different internal and external weather conditions. It is based on the relationship between the permeabilities of the materials used in the wall construction (which also applies to roofs and floors) and their relative locations in the wall. Permeability is the physical property of a material that indicates how easily vapour can pass through it and, like thermal conductivity, is known for most materials. By carefully selecting the layers of the wall construction so that relatively low permeability materials are toward the inside surface, i.e. there is more resistance to water vapour, and high permeability materials are on the outside, condensation is completely avoided under any set of weather conditions. It is important to realise that there is always some amount of condensation and evaporation taking place in a wall but that problems only develop when there is a build-up of water, in other words when the condensation rate greatly exceeds the evaporation rate. BS 5250 gives this value at something greater than 500 g/m^2 over a 60-day period. Anything less than this would be considered inconsequential. The evaporation rate is helped by insuring that there is good outside air ventilation above the insulation — a general requirement of 50 mm is indicated in the Building Regulations.

Our Construction

Our architects, Keystone Architects, in conjunction with the German company Isofloc, Ökologische Bautechnik, manufacturers of cellulose insulation, developed the particular combination of layers and materials for our breathing wall.

In general terms the permeability ratio of inside board to outside board needs to be at least 5 to 1, the higher the better, i.e. the outside layer needs to be at least five times more permeable than the inside board. Permeability is roughly related to density: more dense materials tend to be less permeable, which would make sense. In our case, the medium board that we use, Karlit sheathing, has a vapour resistivity of 25.74 MN-s/g-m, while the exterior low-density bitumen-impregnated fibreboard has a resistivity of 5.00 MN-s/g-m. This meets the 5 to 1 ratio criterion and condensation is avoided. If the medium board were left out and there were only plasterboard with a resistivity of 10.00 MN-s/g-m, then condensation would occur and the insertion of a vapour barrier would be required. For comparison, the vapour resistance of polythene sheeting is something like 10 to 20 times as great as that of medium board, and that of aluminium foil (as used on foil-faced plasterboard) more than 400 times as great. By using a material like medium board with the minimum required vapour resistance we can get the maximum amount of beneficial exchange of air and vapour without difficulties. Using polythene or foil is effective against condensation but is also an overkill, leading to a sealed-box effect, where the beneficial breathing qualities of natural materials are denied to the inhabitants.

The rate at which this building construction 'breathes', i.e. how many air changes per hour (AC/hr) actually take place through the solid fabric, is unknown at this point. The Martin Centre for Architectural and Urban Studies of the University of Cambridge Department of Architecture did a two-year study, begun in April 1992, on one of our houses. The purpose of the study was to determine how well the wall actually performs both thermally and in terms of 'breathing'. It would appear that the rate of breathing is low and could not be measured in the experimental range, around 1.0 AC/hr. We suspect that the layers of plasterboard and Karlit sheathing are more resistant than claimed. There is some large variation in published values of vapour resistivity, though as more research is being done we expect that they will become more consistent and accurate.

We expect that that actual rate will be in tenths of an air change, less than would occur due to normal air movement. The test house was checked for air tightness and did quite well, about 0.25 AC/hr. Older houses might be as much as 3.0 AC/hr, while a modern fairly well sealed house would be in the range of 0.5-1.0 AC/hr.

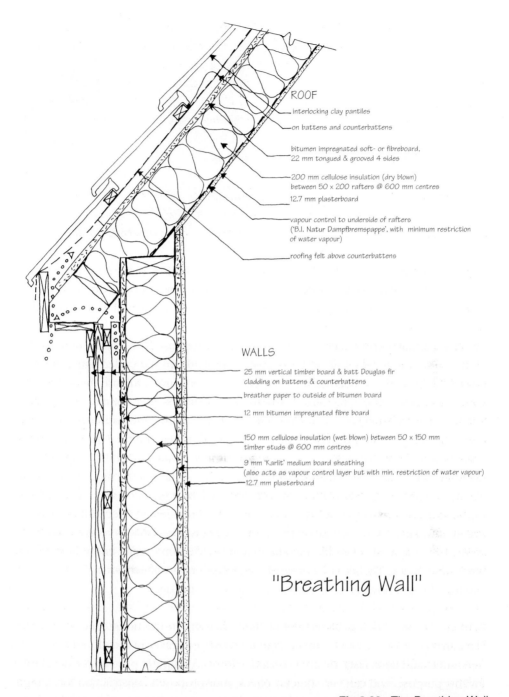

ROOF
- interlocking clay pantiles
- on battens and counterbattens
- bitumen impregnated soft- or fibreboard, 22 mm tongued & grooved 4 sides
- 200 mm cellulose insulation (dry blown) between 50 x 200 rafters @ 600 mm centres
- 12.7 mm plasterboard
- vapour control to underside of rafters ('B.I. Natur Dampfbremspappe', with minimum restriction of water vapour)
- roofing felt above counterbattens

WALLS
- 25 mm vertical timber board & batt Douglas fir cladding on battens & counterbattens
- breather paper to outside of bitumen board
- 12 mm bitumen impregnated fibre board
- 150 mm cellulose insulation (wet blown) between 50 x 150 mm timber studs @ 600 mm centres
- 9 mm 'Karlit' medium board sheathing (also acts as vapour control layer but with min. restriction of water vapour)
- 12.7 mm plasterboard

"Breathing Wall"

Fig 2.22 The Breathing Wall

The Martin Centre tests did prove two important facts though. First is that the insulation technique of blown cellulose does perform well thermally. Second is that the walls remained dry and after a year of monitoring showed no indication of any condensation, reassuring the skeptics who may have been concerned about moisture entering the building fabric.

So the question remains open as to how much benefit the 'breathing' aspect of the fab-

Fig 2.23
Monitoring equipment for study by
the Martin Centre, Cambridge University

ric really contributes to the healthy environment of the houses. In the more recent houses we have experimented with replacing the medium density fibreboard with a paper membrane that has a lower resistivity but still within the theoretical values needed.

Because the main components of the fabric are wood-based, i.e. the medium board, timber studs, rafters or joists, cellulose insulation (made from recycled paper) and low density fibreboard, the hygroscopic properties of wood are in full use. We are told by Isofloc, Ökologische Bautechnik that because of this in winter conditions there will also be a flow of liquid water in the reverse direction, i.e. from the outside to the inside, on a microscopic level through capillary action. This is because the equilibrium moisture content of wood is higher at lower temperatures, around 16% at 0°C, and lower at higher temperatures, around 6% at 20°C. The outside surface of the timber will absorb moisture while the inside will lose it and there will be a gradual movement of liquid from the outside to the inside surfaces, providing a humidifying effect as the moisture evaporates. This is a nice-sounding theory but we must stress that as yet it has not been verified by any hard scientific documentation, so we don't really know how well it works in practice. The idea of a cycle of water vapour travelling from inside to outside and liquid water flowing from outside in is an appealing one.

In Britain, if you are doing calculations on different wall constructions to meet the British Standards BS 5250, we recommend contacting Roger Leaver of Excel Industries (see References and Book List). He offers a service using a computer programme developed for this purpose, and can very quickly check your proposed construction for compliance. However, it is possible to do the calculations yourself if you are so inclined and can get access to the standard, either through your local library or from the British Standards Institute, or from the equilvalent agency for standards in your country.

There have now been over 200 'breathing wall' buildings built in the UK since we completed the first ones in 1990. Though still novel and not fully accepted by the mainstream building industry, the interest is strong and good research continues to be carried out and further improvements made. We are confident that this kind of construction, using natural materials and methods, is certainly the way forward to create healthier and more life-giving built environments.

Structural System

Background

The 'structural system' is the method or arrangement by which the structural members transfer the loads from the roof and the dead weight of the house, contents and people down to the foundations, i.e. the way the building is held up. In timber house construction using small dimension timber, the main structural members are rafters, floor joists and wall studs. Each is carefully sized to enable it to carry its design load for a given condition. The condition depends on the type of building, the weather pattern in the particular area (which tells us how much load we should allow for snow and wind) and the span or effective height of a member. The Building Regulations give the appropriate design values (including references to British Standards in this country). Building Control Officers from the local authority strictly monitor the structural integrity of a building and can request a Design Certificate from a structural engineer if they have any doubts.

In a traditional pitched roof building the most common type of construction is to have the plain rafters placed against each other at the ridge, sometimes using a ridge board, and tied at the bottom end at the wall head with a joist. Often the joist forms the floor support for an additional living area, although the usable area is limited because of the loss of room height at the sides of the house. This is the half storey of $1^1/_2$ or $2^1/_2$ storey houses. Because the rafters are at an angle and carrying the weight of the roof, they have to be restrained to keep them from pushing out at the wall and falling down. The walls don't have the strength in that direction, so something is needed to oppose the pushing out force and the joist is the perfect answer. The price is that some floor area upstairs is lost.

In our case we wanted to make the most of the floor area upstairs and so we raised the roof above the first floor level, making the house effectively two-storey with only slightly higher walls. The result is that the structural system is more complicated.

Our Experience

We have tried several different systems to accommodate the extra height of the walls and our attempts have evolved into a hybrid system we have dubbed the modified post and beam. A brief history to show its evolution will give a better understanding.

1. Cantilever Wall Stud, Ground Beams with Pier Foundations

The first house was probably the most difficult to build and involved the wall studs being made strong enough to take the extra thrust of the rafters on their own. The process was complicated by the fact that the span for the floor joist was too long to run parallel to the rafters (5.2 metres) so the tensile force was taken up between

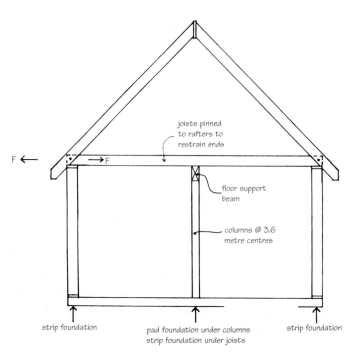

Fig 2.24
Structural section —
'Cornerstone'
(third to be built)

joists pinned
to rafters to
restrain ends

F

F

floor support
beam

columns @ 3.6
metre centres

strip foundation

pad foundation under columns
strip foundation under joists

strip foundation

the wall studs at the first floor level by a combination of steel straps and the plywood subfloor. Plywood was needed here as a stress skin; medium board could not be substituted in a floor application as it does not have sufficient tensile strength. The junction at the rafter stud was also very awkward, with the rafter requiring to be fitted into a U-shaped heavy-gauge steel strapping.

The structure was further complicated by large timber ground beams that spanned between mass pier foundations. The building as a whole used far too much timber because of the various complications but it will no doubt last through the most severe wind storms and earthquakes.

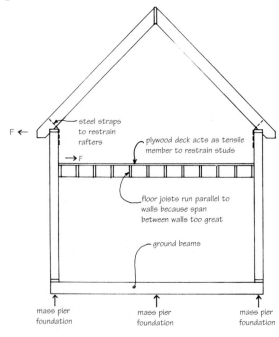

steel straps
to restrain
rafters

F

plywood deck acts as tensile
member to restrain studs

F

floor joists run parallel to
walls because span
between walls too great

ground beams

Fig 2.25
Structural section
House No. 5
(first to be built)

mass pier
foundation

mass pier
foundation

mass pier
foundation

2. Twin Purlin, Ground Beams with Pier Foundations

In the second house we continued with the pier foundations, mainly because we had already poured them before learning of the difficulties associated with the ground beams, but we did eliminate the cantilever wall studs. Instead we used larger timber beams to support the rafters, themselves supported by the gable walls on the ends and by interior walls inside the building. The beams were made up of several pieces of 50 mm timber, in varying depths depending on the span. These are called purlins and run parallel to the ridge and perpendicular to the rafters. With the purlins taking the downward load of the rafters closer to the middle of the structure, the outward thrust of the rafters is eliminated and no special strapping at the wall head is needed.

In this house the floor joists again ran perpendicular to the rafters because of the length of the span (5.2 metres) and the desire to keep the dimension of the joists reasonably small (200 mm). This was not ideal as they then contributed very little to the overall stability of the building, and again plywood was needed in the first floor construction to provide this.

This was an 'L-shaped house with a smaller wing. The ludicrousness of using pier foundations was driven home by the fact that we needed 26 of them for this relatively small dwelling. The excavation looked like an exploded minefield, and because of the dry, sandy soil the sides caved in whenever we walked within a few feet of the edge. It was not a fun experience for our builders and we firmly abandoned the concept.

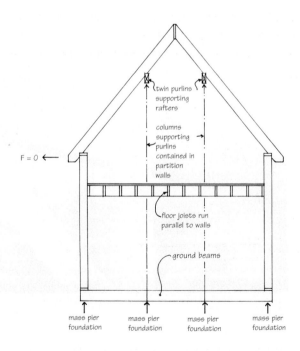

Fig 2.26
Structural section,
House No. 6
(second to be built)

3. Traditional 11/2 Storey, Floor Support Beam and Strip Foundation

In our third house we tried to simplify as much as possible and ended up with (surprise!) a traditional $1^{1}/_{2}$ storey house, with the first floor joists parallel to the rafters and acting as tension members. The only complication was that the span of 5.2 metres was too long for the 50 x 150 mm joists we wanted to use. So we introduced a floor support beam in the centre of the house to support the first floor joists, which was in turn supported by interior walls. We eliminated the pier foundations in favour of much simpler strip foundations, widening the centre strip into pads to allow for the extra loading where the beam was supported. This was very successful, but had two implications. The first was that in using strips blockwork was also required and that meant we needed a skilled bricklayer. The second was that the room upstairs was quite a bit smaller than in the first two houses, for the reasons mentioned earlier. The beam turned out to be rather large (150 x 300 mm) so we dressed it and left it exposed as a feature. See Fig 2.24.

4. Load-Bearing Ridge Beam, Floor Support Beam, Strip Foundations

In this variation a central spine of load-bearing members — the ridge beams and first floor support beams together with the columns — takes the load down to a strip foundation with thickened areas for the columns. The frame is made up of three bays or sections of the house where interior walls can be located. In some places the columns are left exposed as a room feature. Knee braces, held in place with traditional oak pegs, add strength and stability and make attractive internal features. Because the joints are exposed in the living areas we used scarf joints over the posts, providing better bearing strength and an aesthetic appearance.

Fig 2.27
Knee brace and scarf joint
in floor support beam

The exterior walls are normal timber stud work, 50 x 150 mm at 600 mm centres, which is why the system is a hybrid.

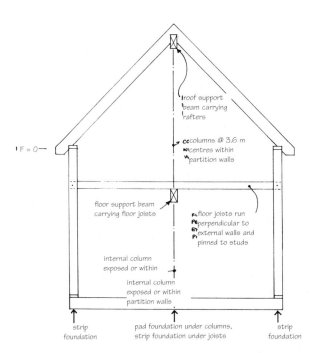

Fig 2.28
Structural section,
House No. 4
(fourth to be built)

roof support beam carrying rafters

columns @ 3.6 m centres within partition walls

F = 0

floor support beam carrying floor joists

floor joists run perpendicular to external walls and pinned to studs

internal column exposed or within

internal column exposed or within partition walls

strip foundation

pad foundation under columns, strip foundation under joists

strip foundation

Because the house is tall, over seven metres, the walls on the south gable end needed extra let in bracing for racking strength against wind, which was easily accomplished by placing diagonal braces in the wall framing. Otherwise the racking strength was supplied in the medium board sheathing on the inside of the studwork.

The beams were made up of 50 mm thick pieces and so we did not have the problem of obtaining large dimension timber. Beams were made up on the ground and lifted into place by hand. Jointing was also done on the ground and, with the beams being generally three pieces thick, voids for the tenons in knee braces and columns could be cut out easily before the beam was assembled, reducing what would normally be a fairly skilled job when using solid timber to one that can be done by a novice with a hand saw, as long as they get the dimensions right!

Fig 2.29
Cutting scarf joint

Because we developed this system ourselves there were a lot of little details that we hadn't thought of that made framing and some of the finishing work more difficult.

For instance we used steel base plates to anchor the columns to the foundations and these were made up on the assumption that the timber dimensions were accurate. This turned out not to be the case, meaning that often we had either to pack out the shoes for a tight fit if the wood was undersized or to chisel out space if it was over-sized. The internal columns often were larger than the thickness of the wall which meant they were proud of the plasterboard. We have not yet found a good detail for finishing the edge between the dressed timber column or beam and the taped, filled and painted plasterboard. Inevitably the timber will shrink and show a crack in the plaster edge.

Although there have been minor problems in the detailing, we are happy with this current system. It has simplified the construction immensely and we are continuing to use it.

In the turf-roof houses started in 1991, where the roof loads are enormous — the weight of the Guest Lodge roof being over 75 tonnes — we used the twin purlin system with strip foundations widened at the columns. It seems to be standing up well, so to speak — at least so far.

Building in the Round

Whilst the first ecological houses we built were of a traditional form, pitched roofed and rectilinear, we continue to develop our own tradition of round or multi-sided buildings that continue to fascinate and delight. In our original brief for the Bag End houses we had become slightly jaded with round. We had experienced them being more complex and taking a long time to build. We thought that square would be faster and more practical. Now with the experience of 11 of these more traditionally shaped buildings which have been erected in the last 5 years, we can say that this is not necessarily so! What we have learned is that the time it takes to build does not really have much to do with the shape or form of the building (so long as it is properly designed and detailed!). It is much more a function of the skill level of the building crew.

Fig 2.30 The fourth variation of the whiskey barrel houses with sandstone base

This may seem obvious to most but it took quite a few years for us to discover this. We have also built a few more round buildings and incorporated all the ecological features, including the 'breathing wall' and solar and energy conservation features. Detailing and structural design are the keys to making the building easy to build, and in a round structure they can be made easy. We certainly experienced the difficulties of awkward detailing in round buildings, but we also had the same experience on rectangular ones! This was a surprise.

Most recently we built two further 'whisky barrel' houses which took about the same time to build as square ones. There is something quite magical and special about round shapes and it is difficult to try to explain or quantify. I am sure we will continue to build both square and round depending on what people want, without any preconceived notions of how easy or difficult it might be due to shape. Design it well and it can be easily built! Find a skilled carpenter/building team and it doesn't have to take a long time . . . . and if you want to use your own labour or other perhaps semi- or unskilled people, which, of course, is also fine and can still produce beautiful results, be prepared for it to take longer!

Fig 2.31   The latest two-storey, double-barrel, breathing wall barrel house

Section 3
MATERIALS

Introduction

By adhering to the Building Biology principle of using materials that are unadulterated or as close to their 'natural' condition as possible, we can minimise or eliminate the effects of artificial toxins. Hopefully we can also avoid high-tech manufacturing methods that require large energy input and polluting processes. The less we have to do to the materials before using them the better, knowing that they have to perform their functions over the reasonably long life of the building. Apart from the energy needed to produce building products, there are also other considerations: air and water pollution; other materials and compounds that might be added and their respective sources; and the overall environmental impact in production.

Some natural materials do require processing and take a fair amount of energy to produce but are still the best ecological choice because of other factors such as longevity and inherent properties, e.g. the ability of copper to conduct electricity without corroding and to carry water without polluting (but not at the same time, of course).

Along with considering the 'natural' aspect of any building material, probably the next most important question to ask is 'Where does it come from?' The simple principle we work with is to look around and see what is available to us locally, for not only will we support the local economy by using it but we will also eliminate large amounts of energy-use and pollution in transportation. This includes locally produced materials as well as grown, harvested or mined ones.

Fig 3.1
Local sandstone quarry at
Hopeman, Moray

It doesn't always work out that local is the best option, such as in our case with sheathing board. We have a plant just 10 miles down the road that produces sheathing grade boarding using softwood timber from local forests that are well managed. But unfortunately it is bonded with large amounts of urea- and phenol-formaldehyde glues, which can outgas into the building and cause health problems. So instead we import sheathing board from Sweden and Norway that uses no toxic glues. It is also a similar price. But in the process of transport we cause more air pollution and global warming! It is always a balance . . . .

Fig 3.2
Ekkehard Weisner, Architect

What has nature provided us with locally and how can we utilise it? Initially we should check out some basic and obvious things like the geology of the area and the available types of local stone; working stone quarries and their products (building stone, aggregate, roofing materials like slate, etc); forests producing timber; local sawmills, and manufacturing plants and their products. Some types of soils lend themselves to rammed earth construction, while others, especially clays, can be used either baked or with minimal treatment in certain types of wall construction. The techniques for these types of construction are specialised and need to be studied and understood thoroughly before being attempted, but an increasing number of alternatives are being developed.

There are usually a myriad of possibilities. One suggestion to help get started is to find a seasoned builder of the old school who remembers building before the age of cheap fuel and before massive amounts of man-made products were available. Or someone who specialises in restoration. They will know what is available around your area, as well as its cost, the best methods for using it, and probably the answers to most other questions you can think of. If you can't find someone like that, don't worry. You will just have to think and experiment for yourself!

Timber

Background

Oe of the best 'natural' materials available for building is, of course, timber. It is generally widely available and requires relatively small amounts of energy input to process and transport. It has good strength properties in tension, compression and bending, is lightweight and is usually relatively cheap. It can be a renewable resource if taken from properly managed forests which, if not over-harvested, will provide us with timber for endless generations. It is also one of the most benign materials to live with, provided it isn't treated with toxic preservatives. According to the checklist of criteria developed by the Building Biology Institute, it rates highest in every area of ecological concern and is the basic yardstick by which we can measure the relative ecological soundness of other materials and products. See Appendices A and B for specific information.

In the global environmental and economic context, the case for using timber for building stands up well (no pun intended). As well as providing jobs, amenity value, wildlife habitat and erosion protection, trees also counteract global warming by absorbing carbon dioxide and tying it up for the duration of their working life, which would normally mean a growth, cutting and use cycle of at least several hundred years.

Fig 3.3
Douglas Fir forest

There are, of course, many types and grades of timber: hardwoods, softwoods, native and non-native species, home-grown or imported, tropical and temperate, each with unique properties and characteristics. Care needs to be taken to identify the source of timber to avoid practices that are environmentally destructive, like the clearing of tropical or temperate rainforest, or the use of rare or endangered species. Friends Of The Earth produce *The Good Wood Guide* which is an excellent reference to check out timber types and sources, both for endangered tropical species and for sustainable softwood and hardwood alternatives. Information is also available from the Ecological Trading Company, 1 Lesbury Road, Newcastle upon Tyne NE6 5LB, UK.

Timber is one of the most flexible, forgiving and easy-to-use building materials, and any house or building, 'ecological' or not, is likely to contain a considerable quantity of it. If produced sustainably, with 'sustained yield' management, timber is a totally renewable resource. 'Sustained yield' simply means that the timber harvested each year never exceeds the amount of new timber growth in a particular forest. If it is locally grown, very little energy is needed to process and transport it. You should research the types of timber available, whether they are hardwood or softwood, native or non-native, what their best uses are, the range and variety of species and the local harvesting practices in order to determine which timber is suitable to use and the best type of construction. Forests with a mixture of species as opposed to a monoculture crop present the ideal situation. With different types of trees yielding wood for a wide range of uses, the varied species provide a healthier balance within the forest itself, creating a more diverse wildlife and plant habitat that has a lower susceptibility to insect and pest damage.

Timber frame construction, where small dimension timber is used to build stud walls, supporting floors and roofs, is widely used in northern Europe, especially Scandinavia, and North America. Post and beam construction, usually requiring larger dimension timber, is also employed widely and is the basis of many old-world building traditions.

Fig 3.4
Wall construction
during building course

In Britain the Forestry Commission has over one million hectares of predominantly conifer forest. Forest Enterprise, a self-contained organisation within the Forestry Commission, is charged with the management of this forest estate owned by the nation. Its aim is to create and maintain attractive and productive woodlands to provide recreational opportunities, wildlife habitat and a constant supply of timber. These forest lands are made up of both the native Scots Pine and non-native species like larch and spruce from Europe, and Lodgepole Pine, Sitka Spruce and Douglas Fir from North America. There are also many private estates that manage forests for timber, particularly in Scotland. Like the Forest Enterprise lands they tend to be almost exclusively conifer forests.

Currently Britain has 10-11% of forest cover, which is double what it was a hundred years ago. The current European average is 25%. When you compare that figure to

Fig 3.5
Timber
store on site

the estimate of original forest cover of somewhere around 95%, it is evident that Britain could easily be self-sufficient for all its timber requirements. Instead, the UK now imports 87% of its needs, or £7 billion-worth annually.

Unlike many countries Britain started its forest management through the Forestry Commission, established in 1919, without vast tracts of virgin or established forest, as most of the original forests were already gone. The initial intention in founding the Forestry Commission was to re-establish a stable supply of timber after reserves had been exhausted during the First World War. Virtually all the timber land that the Commission manages is based on man-made plantations. The increase in forest cover over the past hundred years is in a large part due to the Commission's efforts, though there has also been an increase in plantations on private lands.

Modern forestry placed initial emphasis on fast-growing timber-producing trees and little, if any, thought was given to other uses or possibilities. But in the last decade there has been a growing appreciation within the Commission of the many benefits that tree plantations possess. This has led to the introduction of new ideas and policies specifically designed to create better and more diverse habitats for native wildlife as well as to increase the human amenity value. These include: structuring plantation edges to blend pleasingly with the landscape instead of the unattractive and unnatural straight lines often associated with plantations; leaving areas open and unplanted for the benefit of small mammals; maintaining special areas specifically to attract butterflies and birds; leaving some boggy areas undrained; building ponds or small lakes within the planted area; and creating paths and walks with illustrated signposts to teach people about the workings of nature. In one famous plantation near us at Culbin they have even built 'bat boxes' to encourage and provide homes for a colony of thirty bats.

As a local plantation Culbin is worth a special mention. A series of natural disasters at the end of the 15th century created a coastal dune system that in many ways resembled the Sahara desert. In the early 1920s a heroic effort to stabilise the soil was initiated and this, combined with tree planting, has dramatically transformed a once-barren landscape into a productive and attractive woodland. Though some mistakes were made in the initial planting in the choice of trees, layout and the monoculture style, much has been learned, and the result has clearly been beneficial to both nature

Fig 3.6
Culbin Sands circa 1920.

Fig 3.7
Culbin Sands today
after 70 years of forestry

and humans. The trouble with forestry is that mistakes take a long time to correct, the growth cycle being equal to or longer than a human life span, and many of the defects of plantations visible to the passing motorist or hill walker no longer apply to current practices. Miles of Sitka Spruce planted in monotonous square plots and straight lines are a thing of the past. Culbin is now a thriving Forest Nature Reserve and is classed as a Site of Special Scientific Interest, with a myriad of species of plants and wildlife.

Forest Enterprise now requires a landscape plan, or Restructuring Plan, for each of its woodland estates. It has completed plans for 95% of them, with the remainder under way. This is a tailor-made design and long-term management strategy for each particular site, not only to safeguard the timber supply but also to ensure the best land use on all fronts. Certain areas within each plantation are designated for 'long-term retention', meaning that these stands will be left far longer than they would be within the normal harvesting rotation. Older woodlands have particular qualities that younger ones don't have, with a greater variety of age, species and habitat that naturally evolve given time. For this reason it is important to distinguish between natural forests left to grow and evolve without human interference and those planted to provide us with our timber needs. We must realise that these 'plantations', or managed forests, should never entirely replace the native forests which provide the greatest natural species diversity and ecological stability.

When a section of plantation is harvested, with 400-800 trees per hectare being felled, it is replanted with a minimum of 2,500 seedlings, which are checked for survival two to three years later and replenished if necessary. There is now also a requirement that a minimum of 5% of the trees be broadleaf, the native birch, rowan, wild cherry, hazel and willow being the most common. Some larger species like beech and oak are also used. Forest Enterprise is experimenting with other types of replanting, such as one form of a shelter wood system, where large trees chosen for their quality are left standing to self-seed in a harvested area. Often 40-50,000 seedlings per hectare are the result instead of the 2,500 that would normally be planted in rows. These types of stands have to be 'respaced' after a few years, which is considerable work with no particular financial gain. But there is the possibility that it may be a more effective and less disruptive way of replanting than the normal machine row furrow cutting procedure.

In our case we are fortunate to live in an area that does have abundant plantations, by British standards, producing a sustainable supply of local timber suitable for building. Morayshire is the most forested county in Britain at 25% tree cover, the same as the European average. Approximately 50% of the forests are Forest Enterprise plantations.

Fig 3.8
Tree planting
in the Highlands

It is worth mentioning the controversy now raging in North America over the old growth forests of the Pacific Northwest of the USA and Canada. Timber quality is generally a function of age. A longer growth cycle produces a stronger, better quality wood: the growth rings or grain are closer together and there are fewer knots or other defects. Because old trees tend to be big, using them means that larger dimension timber is more readily available for beams and columns. In young trees, or trees that have been hybridised to produce unnaturally fast growth rates, the growth rings are widely spaced and the wood is much weaker than close grain timber of the same size. It is also more subject to defects, making it inferior in comparison with old trees.

In old growth forests the trees can be many hundreds, even thousands, of years old and the resulting timber quality is high. In the Pacific Northwest, home of the Dou-

Fig 3.9
Broad leaf deciduous forest

glas Fir, hemlock, Western Red Cedar and many other trees, the old growth has been almost completely cut down. Only 10% of the original remains of the world's most productive temperate forest. To get good quality second growth — or replanted — timber, the harvesting cycle has to be sufficiently long to let trees mature and reach a good size. What has happened in this area is that when cutting began no immediate replanting took place, as the natural forests seemed so vast that they would never run out. Cutting cycles need to be at least 70-100 years to produce quality timber and the new cycle simply has not been started early enough. Because of the inferior quality of the timber being harvested from the immature planted or 'second growth' trees there is great pressure to allow cutting in the few remaining old growth stands.

But there is more to a forest than just timber. An old growth forest provides a unique ecosystem that has evolved over millennia and that cannot be replicated in managed plantations with the shorter harvesting cycles that are necessary to fulfil the demand for timber. It has been shown that there are specific animals that require old growth forests for habitat, and to cut those remaining forests down completely would mean those animals would face certain extinction. In a landmark law America has halted the cutting of old growth in the Pacific Northwest on the evidence that one species of spotted owl was being threatened under the Endangered Species Act. This has sparked massive controversy and continuing heavy protest from the forest industry.

Fig 3.10
Old growth forest with mixed ages and species

The lesson from this story is not about the spotted owl but about the need for humans to take a long-term view. In the early 1900s, when much of the forest cover of North America was being logged, there was little or no thought given to future generations. Had the forests felled then been replanted immediately, much of the current difficulty in finding good quality second growth timber would have been avoided. And the remaining old growth forests, a tremendous natural treasure and legacy for future generations, would have remained free from pressure from the logging interests.

Europeans have a much longer tradition in forest management, and Scandinavia in particular has the most thorough and enforced timber harvesting and planting policies.

Sustained yield is not a theory but the minimum requirement and many companies plant substantially more than they harvest. They know that the long-term future of their company, as well as the well-being of the natural environment, depends on it.

In Scotland there are only a few scant remains (approximately 1% of the original range) of the once abundant Caledonian forest, dominated by the Scots Pine. Plantations can never replace these treasures and adequate protection of ancient forests should always be a priority. But though there is no danger of felling for commercial gain, these areas are suffering the effects of human intervention in the natural balance of things in that overgrazing by deer and sheep is hampering natural regeneration. The Findhorn Foundation Community, through its Trees for Life programme, has initiated a project to assist the natural regeneration in some of these remote areas of Scotland through fencing and tree-planting work. For more details please write to: Trees for Life, The Park, Findhorn IV36 0TZ, Scotland.

Timber – Our Experience

The timber available to us here in Moray is good for building, provided you don't mind some varying dimensions and a wide range of moisture content. For the main structural members and for cladding we are able to get Douglas Fir, a beautiful, strong and relatively cheap wood that weathers well and is excellent for exposed beams inside a building. There is also a wide range of rough-sawn mixed spruce, fir and pine used for framing and carcassing timber. Beech, oak and ash are also available in Scotland for finer work like kitchens, cabinets and staircases.

Our local sawmill can supply most of our needs provided we give them enough lead time. And we can have the timber exactly as we want it, from special sizes and profiles for cladding to larger dimension beams for special structural applications. As well as Douglas Fir we use local timber for joists, rafters, wall plates and studs, structural columns, carcassing, flooring, fascia, soffits, roof tiling and wall cladding battens, interior trim and finish work and sometimes for sarking, in the case of the turf roofs. We have also used softwood white pine flooring.

Fig 3.11
Local saw mill and
timber supplier

We have had some difficulties, however, in that we started out using rough-sawn or 'off the saw' timber. The dimensions were sometimes 5-10 mm out, which led to hard times and many headaches for the builders doing the finishing work. After building seven houses we discovered that we can have the timber 'regularised', or put through dimensioning machines, as well as kiln dried, to make cladding, sarking and plasterboarding much easier. This costs an extra 5% but saves time and increases job enjoyment for all concerned.

Our experience with using softwood flooring has been less than totally successful and we are now looking at alternatives. Softwood marks fairly easily and extra care has to be taken, which generally means that houses with pine floors are 'shoes off' homes — fine if you don't mind taking off or putting on your shoes every time you go in or out, as happens in Scandinavia where softwood floors are very common. We have also had trouble with shrinkage and even cupping of floorboards in the relatively short period since the first houses have been completed. It seems that as a subfloor, which is its more normal application here, it will still make sense, but that as a finish floor it is not durable enough.

Because of our policy of using only non-toxic materials, we want our timber to be untreated. Untreated timber can sometimes be difficult to get from commercial builders' merchants, the popular trend being that the more chemically treated a piece of wood is the better. Most builders still insist on fairly heavy duty treatment, usually using a lindane- or pentachlorophenol-based pressure- or vacuum-impregnated process. These chemicals are particularly unpleasant as they have a high content of volatile solvents which evaporate and may then be breathed in. Handling, cutting and building with timber treated this way is a nasty experience. Headaches, nausea and general malaise often result, and we have had first-hand experience of it.

On our first house the structural timber arrived the day before our three-week self-build course was to begin. It arrived absolutely dripping with toxic preservative, having mistakenly been treated despite our order for untreated timber. In the first group meeting on the course we discussed with the trainees, mostly members and associates of the Findhorn Foundation, what to do: whether to use the timber as it was or send it back and cancel the course because it could not be replaced in time. In the end we decided to use it, as the damage was already done and it was going to be used somewhere in the world anyway. The physical reactions that most of us had, despite wearing protective gloves and masks, were enough to convince us of the importance of not using this stuff, and that the arguments against the use of wood treated with toxic and generally nasty chemicals are certainly valid.

Some form of protection for timber exposed to the weather is needed to prevent rot and ultraviolet decay. We use preservatives from organic sources that are certified non-toxic. These tend to provide not so much a 'chemical' protection as a 'natural' one, using ingredients that are found in plants and trees which penetrate and interact with wood to give good resistance to rot and degradation. (See Section 3.10.)

Fig 3.12
Softwood timber floor,
"Meridian"

Obviously in our experience the use of timber has worked well, and we will continue to use it as our main material as long as we can be assured of sustainable sources.
There are many places in the world where timber is not available sustainably and
other types of construction must be used. But there is no doubt that nature will
always provide another resource to give us the materials we need for housing.

Stone

Background

Stone is a wonderful, naturally abundant building material, which gives a special texture and feel to a house either inside or out. Few materials are as beautiful and add as much life, variety and character to a building. In Britain and in fact all over Europe stone buildings have added immensely both to the landscape and to the rich architectural heritage. The English country village — each county with its unique stone as the main building material — is a picture of harmony with nature. Whether of flint or sandstone, slate or limestone, buildings made with a material that comes from land nearby, literally out of the earth, seem to possess a magic all their own.

Fig 3.13
The Nature Sanctuary,
first turf roof and local stone
building in the round

Unfortunately, the skill of stonemasonry, once one of the principal building trades, has been dying out in recent decades. Using stone as the prime structure now tends to be expensive, since labour costs are high and only a skilled tradesperson can do the job properly. The cost of faced stone, cut and squared into blocks for building, is also very high and so stone is not competitive with other modern materials like concrete block. It is another casualty to the cheap alternatives provided by fossil fuel. Because of the skill it requires, it is not advisable to attempt large-scale stone work, particularly if it is to be load-bearing, unless you have the benefit of someone who knows what they are doing to advise you or work with you.

Having said all that, there are still many other uses for stone that do not require high skill levels and that can add beauty and character to buildings.

Our Experience

Stone in our area is of two main types: granite and sandstone. Both can be used in building and the quarries are less than 10 miles from our site. With our limited resources and skills we decided to use stone mainly in landscape features like pathways, retaining walls, skirting around houses, patios and flower bed borders. The

Fig 3.14
Footpath using local sandstone

granite available, gneiss, is random rubble, not squared or faced but beautifully varied in colour and texture, and at £4/tonne extremely cheap to use.

Sandstone we buy from a local stone cutter in random pieces. Large blocks are sawn and squared leaving off-cuts that are smooth on one side and widely varying in thickness. These make for excellent patio material, sometimes called crazy paving because of the irregular shapes that result.

Stone can also be used inside houses for feature pieces like fireplaces, low sill walls and flooring, and can be used as thermal mass to help to regulate building temper-

Fig 3.15
Stonework,
Universal Hall, 1978

ature. This is particularly important in making use of passive solar gains, since the mass of stone provides added heat storage capacity. Placing a stone feature in the path of the sun, for example in a conservatory, sun space or opposite a large south-facing window, allows it to be heated during the day. It can then gradually release its warmth during the evening and night to help keep the room temperature at a more comfortable level at no extra fuel cost to the owners.

Laying paths and walkways does take some skill, especially in the choosing and arranging of stones to make a harmonious pattern. It is a skill that can be learned reasonably easily but can be quite time-consuming at first. Paths and patios need to be dug out and filled with 50-100 mm of gravel, then a 50 mm layer of sand. The slabs of stone are then arranged in the pattern of your design, levelled and finally the spaces between pointed with mortar. We use a mix of 4:1 sharp sand to cement. Stones need to be washed or sponged carefully to remove excess mortar before it sets but without removing too much from the joints.

Fig 3.16
Mosaic patio
at the Community Centre

Patio design can be enhanced with the use of unusual stones, broken bits of coloured glass, pottery and the like, creating a mosaic effect. Often these things are available for free. The only trick is to make sure the smaller pieces are bedded properly so they don't pop out from the effects of frost and winter conditions. Do spend some time working out your design if you go for a more complicated pattern because you will most likely be looking at it for a long time to come!

Dry stone walling is also a traditional craft that once flourished in Britain. It has enjoyed something of a revival in recent years with training courses offered at colleges. We have been fortunate in having a trained stonemason work with us who has been responsible for creating some wonderful retaining walls and landscape features.

Fig 3.17 Dry stone wall
construction at the
Guest Lodge

Clay

Background

Clay taken directly from the earth could hardly be more natural. It is one of the oldest of building materials, having been used in Mesopotamia over 10,000 years ago. It is readily available in most areas at relatively low cost. In fact about 74% of the hard surface of the earth is either pure clay or laterite, a clay with some iron content. Today more than one third of the world's population live in houses built of clay. It has good air diffusion, thermal storage and hygroscopic qualities, and is generally known as a health-giving substance. Clay is permeable to the earth's electromagnetic field which is naturally present all around us and considered to be beneficial. Other materials, such as those based on concrete and asbestos, block out this field.

In temperate climates clay is usually used in a fired form like bricks and roof tiles, which are more durable and weather resistant and less susceptible to water. Fired clay products are made from what are known as 'brick earths', mixtures of shale and clay laid down as surface deposits in ancient lakes and river beds. Each local area will have its own unique variations in colour and texture due to differences in trace minerals, and when the clay is baked shade variation will also be created in the firing process. These variations add to the interest and beauty of bricks and tiles and make clay a very attractive natural material to use.

Fig 3.18
Pottery products

There are other environmental considerations when using clay products. Because clay is usually taken from surface deposits, the extraction process is quite destructive to the landscape and it is important to find out what the extraction company's policy is regarding restoration and reinstatement of worked areas. Find out where the clay comes from and ensure that you buy from a manufacturer that does deal responsibly with reinstatement. Also investigate the impact of the manufacturing and firing process on workers and the local environment.

Our Experience

In our houses we use interlocking clay pantiles for roofs and vitrified clay pipe for underground drainage. In selecting our roof tiles we called various manufacturers and eventually chose a company that produces its tiles in France. They take great care in the extraction of the clay and only go to a depth of 5 metres. Transplantation of trees and the replacement of top soil is done on a continuous basis. Although we would have preferred to use a tile from a British source, we were not satisfied that enough thought was being given to restoration and environmental considerations by the various companies we contacted. One company said that, although they didn't really have a policy, the holes tended to fill up with water which the birds appeared to like to use. This didn't seem to us to qualify as a 'responsible approach' to environmental restoration!

Fig 3.19
Clay pantiles being installed on "Meridian"

The clay pantiles that we have used are double interlocking and are not as forgiving in location and placement as single interlocking tiles, which have considerable tolerance. This means that great care has to be taken in the setting out of the tiling battens and indeed the entire roof. We have found that it is easiest to design roof lights, dormers and even the length of the building around whole tile widths to avoid cutting. Even the eaves overhang should be adjusted around the tile length rather than taking a random chance that it will all work out. Cutting pantiles is done with an angle grinder and is a messy business, and getting cut tiles to sit properly is not always as straightforward as it might seem. Although it is a little extra work on the drawing board to work out precisely the various roof dimensions, openings, overhangs, etc, it is far less work than having to cut masses of tiles. If you do take the time to do the setting out properly, then the tiling is very quick and easy and it is a real joy to watch your roof go on in a day or two, as opposed to the several weeks it may take with a lot of cutting.

The drainage pipes we use are also made of clay. Clay has been used for more than a hundred years for underground drainage, since the advent of the modern water closet when indoor plumbing was first introduced. The early clay pipe was baked in a kiln and given a salt glazing to form an impervious layer on the outside surface. Modern clay pipe is baked at higher temperatures, between 1050 and 1100°C, which

Fig 3.20
Laying of clay drainage pipes

causes the clay to become more glass-like, or 'vitrified'. The vitrification process forms the impervious layer needed on the outer surfaces. It also strengthens the pipe, making it more robust than its earlier counterpart.

Because of this extra strength pipe walls can be made thinner, saving material. This kind of pipe is also more resistant to chemical attack and high temperatures than its main modern competitor, the uPVC pipe. The strength of vitrified clay is also an advantage over uPVC in that the total strength of an underground drainage system is a combination of the strength of the pipe and the supporting soil or earth around it. A vitrified clay pipe provides 60% of the strength while a uPVC pipe provides only 10%, making the bedding process for a clay pipe much less critical. With uPVC pipe, which is flexible and easily damaged, much more care must be taken in selecting and laying of backfill, ensuring proper compaction and support. Clay pipe is more robust and, as a result, is less sensitive to improper installation, though care should still be taken to follow the manufacturer's recommended procedures.

Clay for the pipes we use comes from quarries in North Yorkshire, owned by the manufacturing company. It consists of lower carboniferous shales and mudstones taken from up to six sources all within 5 or 6 miles of the factory and blended to give the right composition. The clay is taken out in narrow strips, usually from outcrops of the clay soil, on a rotational basis around the quarry, with the overburden being put back into the strips and grassed over again, maintaining the land's natural contours.

Insulation

Background

There are many types of insulation available today, ranging from the more common man-made mineral wools (fibreglass and rock wool) to more exotic materials like cork and vermiculite. There are many factors to consider when choosing your insulation: the cost; the relative effectiveness (thermal properties); the stability and life of the material; the practical considerations of how it is fixed or installed — as well as environmental and health concerns regarding exposure to it of installers and residents. Here is a short list of the more common options and their sources. There are roughly three main categories: organic materials from natural vegetation; organic materials from fossilised vegetation (petroleum or coal); and inorganic materials from natural minerals.

Natural Vegetation

General properties: Comes from renewable sources; carbon-based; combustible; needs chemical treatment to resist fire, vermin and rot; use limited by regulations; simple production techniques; relatively low price and low performance; has been used for a relatively long time.

Cork: A light, thick, elastic outer bark of the Mediterranean Cork Oak tree.
Straw: The hollow stalks of grain after threshing.
Woodwool: Strands of wood bonded together with cement and pressed into slabs to form rigid boards.
Fibreboards: Finer wood fibres bonded together loosely and pressed into boards. Less rigid and less dense than woodwool.
Cellulose: The main substance making up the cell walls or fibres of plants. In practice this means wood and the insulation is usually made from recycled paper.

Fossilised Vegetation

General properties: Carbon-based synthetic polymers; combustible; vermin and rot proof; stability varies, some known to outgas; fire resistance varies but most give off toxic fumes; price and performance vary.

Expanded polystyrene: A tough plastic made from synthetic polymers and expanded to form either loose beads or boards.
Extruded expanded polystyrene: Expanded polystyrene that is further extruded giving it extra moisture resistance and higher insulation value. It is sometimes called 'closed cell' polystyrene.
Polyurethane: A synthetic rubber polymer usually used in board form, though it can be in foamed form, e.g. for use in cavity walls.

Inorganic Natural Minerals

General properties: Silicon or calcium based; incombustible; vermin and rot proof; relatively stable; relatively permeable; medium price; medium performance.

> *Mineral fibres (fibreglass and rock wool):* Spun glass or rock bonded with glue and available in quilts, mats and rigid and semi-rigid slabs.
> *Perlite & vermiculite:* Lightweight volcanic rock that when heated expands, trapping air and making a good loose fill insulation. Can also be used in light-weight cement screeds.
> *Foamed glass:* Expanded cellular glass, inert, expensive and with mainly specialised use.
> *Foamed concrete:* Precast concrete blocks and slabs with high level of entrapped air. Also known as lightweight concrete.

The most common insulation materials used today are fibreglass, rockwool and polystyrene and although they are reasonable insulators, they all have their drawbacks. Mineral wools are unpleasant to work with (they are classed as irritants and possible carcinogens) and, to help them hold their shape, they contain resins and glues made from some of the nastier binding agents. Polystyrene is made from petrochemicals and some manufacturers use CFCs as the blowing agent (the most damaging of the ozone-attacking chemicals), though most now claim to be ozone-friendly.

In the renewable category by far the best choice is cellulose. It has good insulating properties and thermally it actually out-performs mineral wools, being roughly equal to polystyrene. It is classed as non-toxic and non-irritant and, though dusty when blown, is not unpleasant to work with. It does require some special blowing equipment and is not as easy to use as the minerals wools and rigid boards in that regard. It is relatively inexpensive and is stable when treated (with non-toxic chemicals). Other renewables, like cork and wood, are not nearly as good insulators and can be quite expensive in the quantities needed to reach high insulation levels.

Our Experience

We chose cellulose as our primary insulation and have been very satisfied with its performance. Cellulose has been used for many years in lofts and floors where it would lie flat and any settlement would be minimal. With recent advances in application techniques, cellulose can also be applied to walls, i.e. in vertical situations. Previously that wasn't possible as the dry-blown material tended to settle over time causing gaps in the insulation and cold bridges at the top of walls.

Through Keystone Architects and our own contacts we learned of an insulation company in Germany using a wet-blown technique. The technology was actually developed in North America and has been used successfully for over ten years. Basically the dry cellulose is emptied from bags into a hopper where it is agitated to fluff it up (giving a higher air content and better insulation value) and then pumped through a long flexible hose to where the insulation is being applied. At the nozzle there are two fine-mist water sprays that dampen the cellulose just enough to cause it to 'stick' to the wall. It behaves a bit like papier-maché and when dry becomes fairly rigid, avoiding any settlement.

Once the cavity between the studs has been filled, the excess is trimmed off neatly with a rotary brush fitted to an electric drill. The excess insulation, or overspray, is then swept into the joist spaces and used for floor insulation. This process does require the stud wall to be clad on one side to give the insulation something to stick to, and it takes a few days to air dry before the open side of the wall can be clad.

Fig 3.21
Wet-blown cellulose
insulation being applied

Fig 3.22
Trimming the overspray of the
cellulose insulation from the studs

Fig 3.23
The finished wall airdrying for
several days after spraying

Environmentally speaking, we feel that the other options for insulation don't really come close to cellulose. It is made from recycled paper, is renewable, non-hazardous to use and inexpensive. We did have our challenges with learning how to use the blowing equipment with operators who were untrained, and the equipment for doing both dry- and wet-blowing cost nearly £4,000. In the first house we built, begun in March 1990, we made the mistake of trying to blow the cellulose from the outside, fighting the wind and rain all the time and eventually constructing large polythene tents round the scaffolding. We wasted a lot of material in the process and had a horrendous time trying to work around the blowing operation with all the other building jobs going on at the same time. The neighbourhood to the lee-ward side of the house looked as though a grey snow storm had struck. Also, since we started our project, there are now a number of trained installers around the country with their own equipment who can do the job for you. This is by far the best way to go about wet-blowing cellulose, although for horizontal applications, like lofts, DIY is quite possible.

In practice we have found that using the wet blown method takes considerable skill, usually more than we could muster. Operators do need training to get used to the equipment, find the right water contact and develop the spraying technique. We have generally been spraying walls that are 150 mm (6") thick and we found that this is the limit of wet spraying. In the latest building we went to a higher level of insulation, 200 mm (8") walls, wet spraying was not possible. The mass of the wet insulation becomes too heavy as the top of the cavity is reached and the entire bay has the demoralising habit of falling out en masse on top of the operator. I got to experience this first hand for several days in cold winter conditions. It was not fun.

With equipment improvements it is possible to do dry blowing now in the vertical applications by pumping the insulation into the wall cavity with special wall noz-zles. It does require a different construction sequence and special thought in order to make the blowing easy, but it is quite simple and actually faster and less hassle. Thicker levels of insulation are quite possible to achieve with only a slight disad-vantage in that you can't see that the insulation is in place. On our most recent build-ing we substituted the internal sheathing board with reinforced 'Pro Clima' build-ing paper. The paper was stapled to the stud faces and then supported by timber battens at 300 centres. The paper can then be physically touched and checked it is filled with the right density and compaction. Blowing dry is definitely the amateur's best option. Wet blowing is still quite good for thinner walls but we recommend get-ting a trained operator and not D.I.Y. job.

We were able to check several houses using an infrared video camera and found that we had far more cold bridges from settling insulation in the wet blown walls than in the house with dry blown pumped in walls. We are fairly sure that the little set-tlement that did occur in the wet blown walls was due to operator error more than anything else, as where we didn't have settlement we had had a good operator. But in the dry blown house there was no settlement at all after more than one year. There were a few places where it just wasn't possible to use cellulose and our second choice in those very limited cases was mineral wool. Although it is an irritant and has suspected long-term health risks, it does come mainly from a naturally abundant material, i.e. rock. It is manufactured from volcanic rock to which limestone and coke are added. The molten material is spun into wool which is then resin-impregnated to help it hold its shape. In our experience mineral wool is somewhat easier to cut and fit than fibreglass, and seems to be slightly less irritating to use, although there is not much to choose between them. It is denser than fibreglass, giving it better sound-proofing properties.

Composite Boards/ Sheet Materials

Background

Modern construction uses much in the way of sheet goods, like plywood, chipboard, wafer board, MDF (medium density fibreboard) and plasterboard, which makes building easier and faster. In timber construction studs, joists and rafters are set out at convenient spacings, usually 600 or 400 mm, to take the standard size sheets, normally 1200 x 2400 mm, and sheets can be put in place with little, if any, cutting and/or wastage. This is a good thing in terms of the efficient use of materials. The only difficulty from the green point of view is the high level of toxic glues found in most sheet goods. Urea- and phenolic-formaldehyde can make up as much as 10% of the average sheet of particle board, MDF or plywood.

These modern boards, the so-called pressed wood products, are the major source of formaldehyde in homes. In their manufacture excess formaldehyde is used in the formaldehyde resin mixture to speed up the curing process. The extra, or 'free', formaldehyde never forms a chemical bond with the wood or resin, but simply sits in the air pockets in the boards, waiting to find its way eventually into the indoors air. It is this phenomenon, known as outgassing, that makes these types of composite boards so notorious as a source of indoor air pollution. In Germany there is now a rating system for assessing the formaldehyde content of different products and through simple labelling it is possible to determine whether a product is formaldehyde-free, or in what range of content it is. As the information about formaldehyde spreads we will no doubt have this kind of system introduced in Britain.

Fortunately, there are alternatives. We have located a manufacturer of 'medium board' and low-density fibreboard that uses no binding agents other than the natural lignin found in wood.

Our Experience

Karlit Medium Board: This product is equivalent in racking strength to plywood and can therefore be used in place of normal sheathing plywood to give the structural stability needed in a timber house. It is made from waste wood materials — sawdust, wood chippings and thinnings — and when these are mixed with water, heated and compressed, the lignin they contain (the substance that holds wood fibres together in trees) is rebonded to the wood fibres. Medium board does not have the same strength in bending and tension as plywood and so isn't suitable for flooring. Nor does it have any resistance to water and cannot be used in places where it could come into contact with moisture. It is available only in 9 mm thickness and has a density of 725 kg/m³, and so is fairly stout.

The fact that the medium board is made from waste material that otherwise might be thrown away and that it contains no formaldehyde or other toxic-based glues makes it one of the 'greenest' mass-produced products we could have imagined. It is also an integral part of the breathing wall construction, described in the Construction section. It does require energy to manufacture and, because it is not currently available in Britain, we import it from Sweden, which means extra energy for transport.

The only real difficulty we have encountered is its moisture-absorbing aspect. In the application of our wet-sprayed cellulose insulation, the insulation should be allowed to air dry for several days before the medium board is applied. But in several cases we were in too much of a hurry and put it on while the insulation was still quite damp. This led to the medium board warping, creating some lovely, relatively unobtrusive wavy patterns after the plasterboard was applied. In some cases the plasterboard nails pulled through the paper and we were forced to go back and re-nail it or use screws. Apart from that, there is no particular problem other than a visual one if you are not rigidly inclined toward straight lines. This would not have happened had we waited the normal time period or if a dry insulation had been used.

Fig 3.24
'Karlit' sheathing board

Fibreboard: Bitumen-impregnated low-density fibreboard, or softboard, is another product we use extensively and is produced in much the same way as medium board. It is much less dense (270 kg/m³) and is impregnated with bitumen in the pulp stage of the process to give it resistance to water penetration. It is used on the outside of studwork, under the ground floor joists and on top of the rafters. Again, as it uses waste materials and no formaldehyde-based glues, it fits the environmentally-friendly requirement. Bitumen, however, is not a particularly nice substance. It has several sources but most is made through the distillation of coal tar or petroleum, although it can also occur naturally in the form of asphalt. During building construction the fibreboard is exposed to potential water damage either while being stored on site or on the stud frame before cladding is applied, so it needs the protection of something like bitumen. The bitumen content is usually around 10-12% and although the substance is not as toxic as formaldehyde and does not outgas in the same way, using this kind of fibreboard is a compromise. However, because the boards are always placed on the outside of the wall, roof or floor construction, any possible contact with indoor air is minimised.

Fig 3.25
Celit 4-D board,
bitumen board roof sarking
with profiled edges

There is a wide range of thicknesses available, from 8 mm to 25 mm. It is also highly permeable to air and water vapour which makes it ideal for our 'breathing wall' construction. We use 12 mm square edge board as external wall sheathing and under ground floor joists (needed to hold cellulose insulation in place). But on the roof we use a thicker 22 mm board with specially profiled edges to shed water. It is tongued and grooved on all four sides and can be left exposed for some time without deteriorating.

We have made some compromises in our mainly non-toxic composite board approach. In our first two houses the structural engineer specified plywood for the first floor to act as a stress skin panel, since medium board wasn't suitable. We also use plywood for temporary floors, needing to have a safe walking surface until the permanent floor is in place. This can't be done until the insulation is completed since, with our system, the overspray insulation is swept into the joist spaces. We re-use the plywood for other houses, concrete formwork and other small jobs but it is not the ideal use of materials. In the latest houses we are experimenting with the tongue and groove softwood subfloor being laid first and have eliminated the temporary plywood floor. The floor insulation is then blown in later, lifting floor boards to reach the joist space.

A bigger compromise has been in kitchen units where we have, in several cases, bought in kitchen units made from MDF, one of the worst offenders in terms of formaldehyde content. This has been due mainly to poor planning and inadequate research, the kitchen being one of the last things we thought about. To balance that we have also had the experience of building a wonderful solid hardwood kitchen from local Scottish ash, which was more expensive but well worth it. We are now set up to produce our own kitchen units with the in-house skills and facilities avail-

Fig 3.26
Eileen Caddy's kitchen —
solid ash construction using locally
grown timber

able and, with better advance planning and experience, it has proved quite feasible cost-wise.

There are also kitchen units available made from solid wood if you look for them. Alternatively, you may be able to find a local joiner who can produce a made-to-order kitchen at a competitive price but again this requires better advance planning and a willingness to engage in the design process.

If, as in our case, compromise is sometimes necessary, it is better to use boards with phenol-formaldehyde rather than urea-formaldehyde glues. Phenol glues are more stable than their urea counterparts and will outgas less. Phenol-based glues are usually used in exterior and water-resistant boards, which are generally more durable because of their ability to stand up to some degree of exposure to moisture. Boards with urea-formaldehyde glues have virtually no moisture resistance and are very easily damaged by water, as anyone will know who has seen a piece of chipboard after it has been left in the rain or been soaked by a leaking pipe. The binding power of the glue is broken and the wood particles absorb the moisture like a sponge, causing swelling and loss of strength.

If products like blockboard and plywood are used, it is best to obtain those made of softwood or birch and to avoid the use of all tropical hardwood veneered products. There are some that claim to be from managed forests, but verification is very difficult in Malaysia and Africa.

On the question of whether there is really that much difference between the conventional glued boards and the non-toxic approach, we have had some interesting feedback from our own builders. In one specific case, two carpenters from America arrived to work with us, coming straight from a house-building job where they had been using plywood to sheath the timber frame. Both had been suffering headaches and nausea and had found working with the plywood very unpleasant. Using circular power saws, either hand-held, or the bench or table variety, to cut sheets means that high temperatures are generated by the fast speed of the blade. This causes more toxic fumes to be released than normal, or simply accelerates and/or concentrates the outgassing of formaldehyde. When these two friends arrived we were in the process of sheathing one of our houses and they took up working just as they had been in their previous job, except now they were using our medium board instead of plywood. Both reported that they had no more headaches or nausea and that they were actually enjoying working with this board, as opposed to suffering through the nasty cutting business, which they had assumed just came with the job of plywood sheathing. But even with non-toxic boards dust is a problem and it is best to wear dust masks.

If you do end up having to use plywood or chipboard it is best to cut it with a hand saw if possible, to reduce the effect of heat-induced toxic gas release. Or, if that is not practical, then be sure that you work in a well-ventilated area and wear masks that protect against vapours.

Plaster and Plasterboard

Background

Plaster has been used for the inside and outside finishes of houses for thousands of years. Evidence of its use has been found in the walls of simple huts built around 600 BC in Turkey. There are many different compositions and types of plaster, from the simple mud or lime plaster of those early dwellings to the dense Portland cement and sand plaster used in the rendering of modern houses.

For the purposes of our construction we refer to the plaster used on the interior walls of buildings, either applied by trowel to metal or timber lath in the traditional way, or in the form of common dry wallboard, usually called plasterboard or gyproc. Plasterboard comes in various thicknesses from 9.5 mm upwards and contains a layer of gypsum plaster sandwiched between two layers of paper.

The main component of both is the naturally occurring compound gypsum, found in sedimentary rocks and used in the making of plaster of Paris. It is hydrated sulphate of calcium ($CaSO_4 2H_2O$) and is non-toxic and benign if taken from natural deposits, which is the case with most British manufacturers. It has excellent absorption and diffusion properties, and is a natural 'breathing' material, which is especially important for the inside surface of the building fabric, the area closest to us. It can be left natural, as some plasters have a pleasing appearance of their own and don't need paint or other finishes. It can also be tinted with natural pigments for a range of colours, as well as decorated with designs made when the plaster is still wet. I wouldn't recommend this practice to the uninitiated, however; it's best to leave this kind of work to the artist or craftsman. Traditional plastering is an increasingly rare skill, with drywall/plasterboard techniques providing big savings in time and materials and generally replacing hard plaster. Both are good sound insulators and provide excellent fire protection.

Not all plasterboards are toxin-free, as there are some types of gypsum — those made from phosphogypsum, containing phosphorus — that are actually radioactive. Plasterboard can also contain additives used in the bonding of paper faces and trace amounts

Fig 3.27
Plasterboard, finishing
the joints and nail holes

of mica, limestone and talc. The joint compound used to cover the seam between two boards usually contains a range of nasty chemicals, including our friend formaldehyde. When a dry-sanding process is used, which is a very messy operation, these irritants can be released into the air and ingested. The chemicals in joint compound can continue to outgas for some months after set. There are low-tox joint compounds available, but if you can't find any when you need them, it is recommended that sanding be done 'wet' to keep dust at a minimum and that face masks be worn at all times, with good ventilation provided.

Our Experience

We have used plasterboard on all the houses as the main interior wall finish, painted with organic paints. It makes an attractive, simple and light wall when painted white or an off-white shade, setting off the naturally finished timber architraves, skirting and trim.

The only difficulty we have had with plasterboard is with some of the detailing around exposed timber, where there is a butt joint. We have yet to find a way of finishing the plasterboard edge without resorting to another piece of trim. And occasionally a nail pulls through the plasterboard paper and needs to be repaired with another nail and some joint compound, but this is fairly normal. The only other, more difficult problem has arisen when the medium board underneath absorbed moisture from wet-blown insulation and warped, as described in the previous section. In some places it caused the plasterboard to come loose and require to be re-nailed, or better yet screwed. Self-tapping plasterboard screws are widely used and are generally better than nails. Special cordless electric hand drills are available to speed the fastening and ensure that the screws are at the correct depth, set just below the surface, but not far enough to tear the paper.

Fig 3.28
The finished wall

Hanging plasterboard is relatively easy and can be taken on by the inexperienced. It is best for at least two people to do it, as plasterboard in full 2.4 x 1.2 metre sheets is heavy. Despite it being an easy job we have found that it is the kind of operation that you might just as well hire a professional to do. It does not cost a lot because a good plasterboard-hanging team can do a normal-size house in a day or less. Taping and filling the seams is another task that we prefer to get professionals for, again because it takes so little time and usually ends up being done better.

In the round houses we have built, we hung our own plasterboard on the curve — not easy as they were compound curves — and then had a professional plasterer apply a 'skim coat' of plaster before painting. This covered lots of imperfections in the hanging process and gave a beautiful finish that looks like hard plaster.

Some plasterboard comes with aluminium foil backing as a vapour barrier. If you want to use any kind of breathing wall approach, don't use this type of plasterboard as aluminium is a very effective barrier and will stop any beneficial air or moisture exchange between the room air and the building fabric.

Copper

Background

Copper is one of the most abundant of natural metals found on earth and has been used by humans for something like 10,000 years. As a building material it was first used extensively by the Romans. The oldest existing copper roof is on the Pantheon in Rome built by the Emperor Hadrian in 130 AD. Needless to say when installed properly it is a very long-lived material!

In modern houses the main use of copper has been for plumbing pipes and as the conductor in electrical wires. It is still used in exterior building work, mainly as roof and wall cladding, but also for gutters, downpipes and valley flashings.

Copper is found in its metal state in nature but more commonly in deposits in rocks and other ores. The process of removing the copper and refining it is not a particularly environmentally-friendly one, both in terms of the smelting process, which creates air and water pollution, and in terms of the energy needed to produce it in its final pure form (99.9%). As can be seen from the table in Appendix B, it is one of the highest consumers of energy by weight, ranking only behind aluminium, plastics and single-layer bituminous roof membrane in kilowatt-hours per tonne needed to produce it.

Some of the shortcomings of copper can be forgiven because of its characteristics and qualities. In terms of electricity conduction, only small quantities are required and there is no economical alternative. In plumbing systems also it is superior to most alternatives in terms of length of expected life, corrosion resistance and stability. A building with copper roof or wall cladding can be expected to last far longer than most, at least several hundred years. Copper can also be recycled and used again with only a fraction of the energy needed in its original manufacture. Currently 50%

Fig 3.29
Copper roof,
whisky barrel house

of 'new' copper is actually from recycled material, making it one of the most successful materials to be recycled, which was largely due in the past to its high quality and the relatively high prices paid by scrap merchants. There are improvements being introduced in the production of copper that will reduce polluting side-effects, although these are not in place in all facilities.

There is an environmental cost to be paid in using copper — there is no question about that. But it would seem to be a one-time cost which needs to be balanced against the benefits of the material's long life and stability.

Our Experience

Since there is no real alternative if you want to have electricity, we have used copper wiring in our buildings; we have also used copper for all domestic water piping, both hot and cold. The only place that we have not used it is in some of the heating systems, where we have used plastic pipe. Copper is superior in our judgment, but it is more expensive and difficult to install. We confess to caving in to the recommendations of our local plumber: the quick-fit couplings and flexible pipe were too great a temptation.

The other application of copper has been as roof flashing, around dormer valleys and cheeks, and other valley junctions. We chose copper here mainly because the traditional alternative was lead, which we felt was unacceptable both because of lead's known toxicity and because we were advised against it if we wanted to collect and use

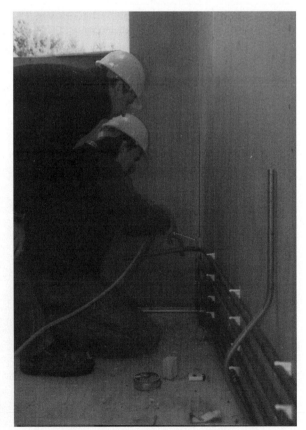

Fig 3.30
Copper pipes for plumbing

rainwater for gardening purposes. Copper is more stable than lead and is less likely to build up in and contaminate collected rainwater.

Because copper is an expensive material, care must be taken when using it to avoid waste. In all three areas where we use it — roofing, plumbing and electrics — a fair amount of skill and knowledge are needed. It is not really a DIY material, although if you are patient, persistent and relatively handy, the skills can be learned. Prior to starting the current ecological houses we did use copper on several roofs, particularly on three 'whisky barrel houses', made from recycled six-metre-diameter whisky vats. We did all the work for the round roofs of these ourselves, and although it was a painfully slow process we did manage it. The result is indeed very pleasing, and in another few years the beautiful light green patina that copper acquires will emerge, which is well worth waiting for.

Turf Roofs

Background

There is a wonderful symbolism in the use of turf or sod as a roofing material: an alive, growing material providing your protection against the elements. Instead of sterile concrete replacing the living soil where a house is built, we simply lift a bit of the soil up and insert a house, putting the displaced sod on the roof and allowing it to live on, nurtured by the rains and the natural processes of life. Each spring we can be surprised at what new seeds have taken root, observing the seasons through the progression of wild flowers and grasses; earth above, earth below. The ultimate in 'green' roofs. Very nice.

Fig 3.31 Turf roof on Youth Building

For the second round of houses that we began in 1991 we decided to try using turf roofs, many of us having talked about their attractiveness for years. The two buildings in question were in a different location from the first houses with clay tiles, and in an area where they would need to be low-profile single storey because of the fine views available. Turf works best on shallow-pitch roofs of 20° or less, so that the soil does not drain too quickly and dry out. Steeper pitches can be successful but they must incorporate intermediate barriers to prevent soil slippage and may require watering. In this location, with part of the brief being to keep the buildings low and non-obtrusive, turf seemed to be an ideal material.

Fig 3.32 Turf roof in traditional style modern hotel complex, Dalarna, Sweden

The main difficulty in using turf is the extra weight imposed on the structure. A normal concrete or clay tile roof construction might be designed to carry 2.0 kN/m² (200 kg/m² or 41 pounds/ft²) whereas a turf roof is closer to 5.0 kN/m² (510 kg/m² or 104 pounds/ft²) for a thickness of 150 mm. That is an increase of some two and a half times. Often turf-roofed, or earth-sheltered/earth-bermed, buildings are constructed of reinforced concrete which is more able to carry heavier loads. In our case, since we are using timber for the main structure, it does mean a fairly large increase in rafter and purlin sizes, but this has also been a tradition in many places in Scandinavia and is certainly not a particularly difficult problem to overcome.

There is some confusion arising from the mistaken belief that a turf roof provides a great deal of extra insulation for a building. There is some benefit but in actual fact it is only 10-12% of the total insulation value at a depth of 150 mm, the majority of thermal insulation still coming from a good thickness of conventional insulation material. Turf provides some extra thermal mass and so has a 'delaying' or lag effect in the cooling down or heating up process, but again it does not make a significant improvement in the overall energy performance.

Another important detail in the use of turf is the waterproofing layer — in other words, how the water is kept off your head, obviously the main function of a roof. If this is not handled competently and the roof leaks, finding and repairing the leak can prove a very difficult task, involving considerably more than a replacement tile, a bit of tar or a piece of flashing. So extra care has to be taken in both the detailing of the sarking (roof deck), eaves and verges, and the drainage and downpipe locations. On the other hand the membrane can have a much greater durability and life because once in place it is protected by the soil from harsh weather conditions, sunlight, etc.

There are quite a few options for membranes, ranging from the low budget three-layer hot-mopped bitumen roofing felt to the high-tech butyl or synthetic rubber sheeting. The thickness of the soil is also an important consideration both in terms of weight and with regard to the plants that will grow in it. As far as the plants are concerned, the thicker the better, to give more room for root growth and provide better water retention. Some designers of earth-sheltered houses recommend as much as 500 mm of soil. It is generally suggested that 100 mm depth is a minimum. In deeper soil a much wider variety of plants and even small shrubs can be grown, whereas shallow soil can only support grasses, succulents and flowers.

There is an organisation in Britain for turf enthusiasts with a fascination for green roofs called The British Earth Sheltering Association. They publish a journal and can be contacted c/o Peter Carpenter, Caer Llan Berm House, Lydart, Monmouth, Gwent NP5 4JJ.

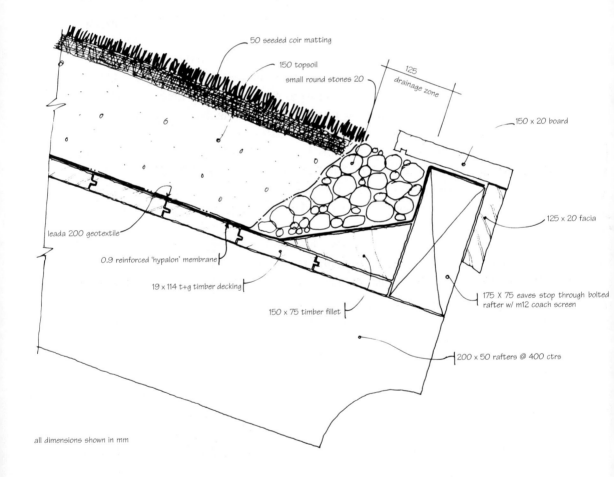

50 seeded coir matting

150 topsoil

small round stones 20

125 drainage zone

150 x 20 board

leada 200 geotextile

0.9 reinforced 'hypalon' membrane

19 x 114 t+g timber decking

125 x 20 facia

175 X 75 eaves stop through bolted rafter w/ m12 coach screen

150 x 75 timber fillet

200 x 50 rafters @ 400 ctrs

all dimensions shown in mm

Fig 3.33   Turf roof: section at eaves

Our Experience

We chose a soil depth of 150 mm, slightly more than the minimum, because of our relatively dry climate (61 cm rain per annum). For the main waterproofing layer we used a single-ply synthetic rubber membrane called 'Hypalon', developed by DuPont over 40 years ago. It is a chlorosulphonated polyethylene reinforced with a polyester scrim for added strength. The membrane is loose laid over a roof deck which must be smooth and free from any sharp objects like nails or other metal fixings. For this reason, as well as the relatively heavy loading, we used 18 x 114 mm tongued and grooved softwood boarding. The t & g boarding made the finished deck fairly smooth and also allowed us to 'secret nail' to avoid any exposed nail heads. We were so meticulous, or possibly paranoid, about getting the roof just right that in some places we even planed the deck where there was a little unevenness in the boards. This was surely unnecessary and, as we found out later, we should have taken more care in getting the ceiling side faces of the rafters aligned where the plaster board is fixed rather than spending so much time on the outside face for the roof deck. In fact the membrane is quite robust and can easily cope with a little waviness in the deck, as long as there are no puncture possibilities. And as the soil goes over the top, no one will ever be able to see the brilliantly straight, smooth and flat deck anyway.

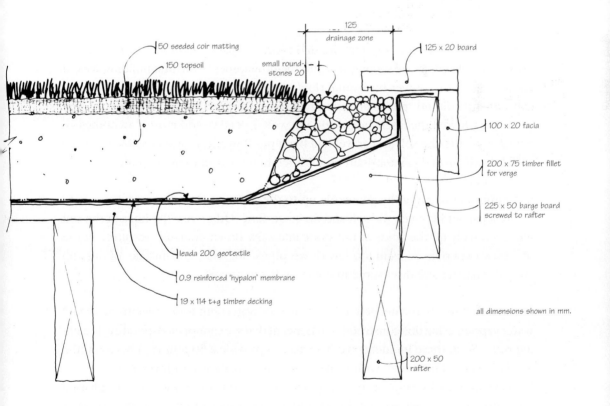

Fig 3.34 Turf roof: section at verge

The actual roof construction is shown in Figure 3.33. Over the membrane is placed a geotextile mat which is needed to keep the soil from migrating down the slope with water movement and to provide a barrier against roots. It is another fairly high-tech product, made from synthetic polymers like polyester and polypropylene which are woven together to form a very tough fleece that is resistant to abrasion, penetration and microbiological attack, while also being permeable. These mats are used extensively in large earthworks projects like road building, revetments and soil stabilisation.

Over the geotextile mat goes the topsoil, which we bought in to ensure good quality. Seeding the soil can be a problem, especially in areas where there are high winds or very exposed conditions. The last thing you want to happen is for your precious, newly seeded topsoil to be blown away into a neighbour's garden. There are alternatives to seeding, like buying in a roll-out grass lawn, which is an expensive but effective method. We chose to use one of a number of available kinds of 'erosion control' matting. Made from organic materials, a combination of coconut fibre, rye straw and cotton wastes and filled with a variety of plant seeds of your choice, the mats are laid out over the topsoil, providing immediate protection and forming a mulching layer that controls weeds. The seeds grow through the mats which, over a period of years, will biodegrade to increase the humus content of the soil. Some mats have a polymer grid that does not break down, to provide extra stability for the soil.

Smooth-edged round stones is used at the eaves and verges to provide better drainage to the downpipes. We have used internal downpipes, i.e. inside the fascia board, using a special inverted 'top hat' welded to the Hypalon membrane and inserted through a hole cut in the sarking and into the downpipe. In the first building we did not anticipate the slower horizontal flow of the rain water through the gravel and consequently did not put in enough drainpipes. During a heavy rain it meant that water overflowed the fascia board and we were forced to add more downpipes — not as easy after the soil and gravel had been put down. It is also possible to install a perforated small diameter drain pipe buried in the gravel to increase the flow.

It is important to bring the geotextile up to the surface before the round stones to create a barrier between the soil and drainage zone. Otherwise the fines in the soil will eventually fill the voids in the stone and slow down drainage, resulting in the overflow experienced from too few down pipes. We made the mistake of not creating the barrier and discovered first hand what happens!

Because the membrane needed to keep the roof watertight is impervious to air and water vapour, using this construction has meant that we cannot incorporate a 'breathing roof'. So in these buildings we have had to provide a 50 mm void between the insulation and the sarking, with vents at the eaves to allow air movement.

We have now had several years of experience with turf roofs and are very pleased with how they are performing. In dry summer conditions there is a need to water the roofs more than an ordinary lawn where the soil depth retains more moisture than the thin layer on the roof. It does not require vast amounts of water but a good soak once every couple of days will keep it looking green. This is not necessary if you don't mind it going a bit brown and dry looking, and we have had a couple of summers when we did not water at all.

We have a number of more conservative residents who are expecting a traditional lawn-like appearance, while others lean toward the 'wild garden' approach. The first is high-maintenance, with someone climbing up and mowing the roof fairly frequently, while the second is low-maintenance, with no mowing involved. At this point we are using the 'hay meadow' theory and cut the growth only once or twice a year, the times being chosen to encourage a wide variety of native wild flowers and a varied look to reflect the seasons. In some parts of Scandinavia it was normal to tether your goat on the roof when the grass needed cutting, but so far we have not tried this, though we haven't ruled out the possibility if we get a few more sod roofs.

With the rising popularity of 'green roofs' there is growing body of knowledge and experience of different types of vegetation, and several companies in the UK have developed a wide variety of choices. We include the names of a number of these in the References section.

In our latest house we experimented with a much thinner layer of soil, intermixed with lightweight aggregate. It is planted with mosses and dwarf grasses which are very low-maintenance, not requiring cutting, and the roof loading is reduced to only about 0.80 kN/m2 . (8.2 kg/m^2 or 16.5 lbs./ft^2)

A little extra work is required to detail the roof for special membranes, as well as deal with the extra weight of the roof in the structure of the building but, all in all, our turf roofs are still quite low cost and attractive and have been very popular with visitors (especially school children who never tire in asking why there is grass on the roof) as well as with community members.

Fig 3.35
Guest Lodge roof:
total weight 75 tonnes

Floors and Floor Coverings

Background

Floors and floor coverings make up a good proportion of the exposed surface area in a house and have an important impact on our overall health and enjoyment of a building. There are many possible materials to use, including natural materials like hardwood, softwood, stone, clay tile, cork tile, linoleum for hard floors and natural fibre floor coverings like sisal, coir (coconut fibre), seagrass and rush matting, as well as wool rugs and carpets.

Most floor coverings nowadays, however, tend to be synthetic: from carpets made from nylon and polypropylene to floor coverings made from vinyl and pvc. These synthetic coverings, mostly petroleum-based, tend to be cheap and easy but unfortunately also contain an amazing number of additives and chemicals that can eventually find their way into our bodies. Synthetic carpets are by far the worst, containing as many as 30 different chemicals, used to prevent everything from mildew to stains, that can and do find their way into the air we breathe. Wall to wall carpets are difficult to clean thoroughly and can be home to a multitude of micro-organisms. There are healthier carpets and rugs, made from wool and available untreated with natural jute backing, although they are more expensive.

Fig 3.36
Floor covering combinations:
wool carpet, hardwood floor
and ceramic tiles

Floor construction can be either single- or multi-layer. In single-layer construction, the main structural floor is also the finished floor, as in a solid softwood or hardwood tongue and groove board that is applied straight onto the floor joists, with the top being finished for wear. There is also a variety of composite boards with veneers used in the same way.

Multi-layer construction uses a subfloor, the structural floor which does not need to be of a high grade for finishing, followed by other layers for sound-proofing, insulation or levelling, with a final floor covering on top. Subfloors can be softwood boarding, chipboard or particle board, plywood or other composite boards made for this purpose.

As all our floors are on suspended timber joists, we concentrate only on that type of construction, though much of what applies will also be true for concrete masonry floors.

Cork — Background

Cork is made from the bark of the cork oak tree that grows in southern Europe. It is a renewable material, in that stripping off the bark does not damage the tree. Once stripped, the tree will then grow a new layer of bark which can be harvested every eight to ten years. The bark is pressed into sheets, and can then be cut into wall or floor tiles or used in larger pieces. It has good thermal and sound-insulating properties and can be used as insulation in the form of corkboard. As thermal insulation it tends to be quite expensive when used in the relatively large thicknesses needed for cooler climates like Britain. Cork is durable and needs very little treatment but when used as flooring does need a protective coating to prevent discolouration from dirt. Generally, wall and floor tiles are quite thin, 3.5 mm thick, so a little goes a long way.

Cork — Our Experience

Our use of cork has been mainly for floors in hallways, kitchens and bathrooms. Because of its insulating properties, it makes a warm floor that is quiet and comfortable to walk on. Since it is such a totally natural product, it is hard to find eco-

Fig 3.37
Cork floor tiles being laid

logical alternatives that compare favourably with it. One thing to watch out for is pre-finished tiles. The finish is generally an acrylic-based product to be avoided. Tiles are always readily available unfinished or natural in most DIY stores or builders' merchants. The best finish we have found, from the health and ecology point of view, is the organic-based floor finish oil and wax system from Auro Organic Paints. It is easy to apply, hard wearing and seems to stand up at least as well as the plastic-based alternatives.

Linoleum — Background

Linoleum is a hard and long-lasting floor covering made from natural raw materials. Linseed oil from the flax plant, resin from pine trees, ground wood from softwood trees (usually from plantations) and powdered cork are mixed with inorganic fillers like chalk and clay and pressed onto a coarse canvas backing. Pigments can be added to give a wide choice of colours and patterns. The pressed material is then cured in drying ovens for a number of weeks giving a resilient and highly durable finished product.

The natural properties of linoleum give it many advantages over other floor coverings: it contains a naturally-occurring bactericide agent which protects it from mildew and germ growth; it is easy to clean and maintain and can be waxed using normal polishes to keep it looking good; it has good thermal and acoustic qualities and helps to reduce noise levels; it is not susceptible to a build-up of static electricity; it is not easily marked or indented, and even burns can usually be removed as linoleum does not melt.

Some manufacturers substitute polyester/glass backing instead of the canvas or hessian natural fibre backing. Both canvas and hessian are very long-lived so if you want the all-natural product be sure to check with the supplier as to which backing is supplied.

Thicknesses range from 2-4 mm. Normally for domestic use 2-2.5 mm is sufficient. Greater thicknesses are needed only for areas of very high wear such as in restaurants and public buildings.

Fig 3.38
Natural linoleum floor

Linoleum — Our Experience

We have not used much linoleum in our houses to date but our experience of using softwood as a finished floor and the problems we have encountered lead us to believe we will be using more in the future, especially with the growing awareness of the health disadvantages of carpet. As can be seen from the description above, linoleum is an ecologically produced and healthy product.

There are only three manufacturers of pure linoleum in Europe: one here in Britain, one in Germany and one in Italy.

Softwood Flooring — Background

Tongue and groove softwood solid timber flooring has been used extensively in Europe and elsewhere as a finished floor for many generations. In Scandinavia it is still the predominant floor for residential housing. The main drawback is that it is soft and is marked easily by anything from furniture to hard-soled shoes. For that reason it has been replaced in many places with floor coverings of various sorts and relegated to a subfloor, the structural part of floor construction that does not need to be seen. Even as a subfloor it has largely been replaced with plywood or chipboard, as sheets are quicker and easier to lay. But despite this softwood is still used commonly.

The usual floor thicknesses range from 19 to 27 mm and board widths from 115 to 140 mm. In traditional building practice in northern Europe, boards are laid down loose for the first year before being nailed, to allow for shrinkage. Flooring should always be ordered kiln-dried, but even at that fairly low moisture content of 12-14% the environment of a heated house will cause considerable shrinkage. The boards should be 'relieved' to prevent cupping. This is done by cutting three to five small grooves on the bottom of the board along the length. Cupping is caused by the way the rectangular boards are cut across the circular growth rings of the log, the shrinkage causing the board to warp into a cup-like shape. The grooves help relieve the differential stress and keep the board from warping.

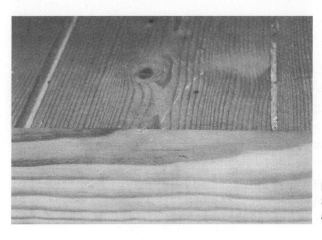

Fig 3.39
Shrinkage of softwood tongue and groove timber flooring

Softwood Flooring — Our Experience

As mentioned in Section 3.01 our experience with softwood as a finish floor has not been one hundred percent satisfactory. Our main difficulty is with shrinkage. Even though great care was taken in putting down the boards, using floor clamps and ensuring they were tight against each other, nailing them securely with a pneumatic nail gun, and doing everything that seemed humanly possible to keep them in place, great gaps opened up after 8-12 months that are now impossible to fix. This error on our part was largely due to not knowing about the old European tradition of leaving the floorboards unnailed for a year. Even with kiln-dried material there will be considerable shrinkage. The shrinkage is greatest in the direction perpendicular to the grain, or across the board. In the one house where we used an unnailed floating floor in one of the rooms we were able to fit in an entire new piece of 140 mm at one wall, and another piece of about 100 mm at the other wall. This means that in one year the shrinkage was 240 mm (10 inches) over the 5.0 metre width of the room. Now we know why the non-nailing tradition came to be!

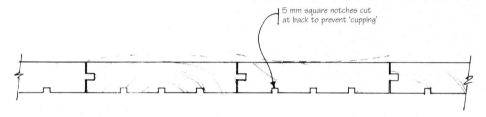

5 mm square notches cut at back to prevent 'cupping'

Fig 3.40   Tongue and groove flooring relieved with grooves on underside

There are other problems, mainly to do with the softness of this type of floor and the need for houses with them to be 'shoes off'. Some people like this idea and for those it is probably a very acceptable alternative. It is a very attractive floor and because of its single-layer construction is very inexpensive. Some people even like the fact that it marks easily, saying that it adds character and charm. But because taking your shoes off is not a tradition in damp Britain, others don't find it so welcoming and prefer a more durable floor.

The cupping difficulty which we experienced in some of the first houses has largely been remedied by adding the relief grooves.

Hardwood Flooring — Background

Hardwood floors are beautiful, durable, warm underfoot *and* expensive. They can be thin or thick solid timber, veneered plywood, blockboard or chipboard, and laid in straight, parquet or herringbone patterns. The variety of wood is large, incorporating a wide range of grains and colours, from beech, birch, walnut, maple, elm and dark and light oak among the native tree species, to acacia, merbau and mahogany in the tropical timber range. We obviously do not support the use of any tropical hardwoods, and given the range and availability of native woods for flooring there is no justifiable reason for using tropical woods.

Fig 3.41
Hardwood strip flooring

The veneered boards have an advantage over solid wood in that they tend not to be as sensitive to moisture conditions and are therefore more stable. The flooring must be at roughly the same moisture level as the atmosphere of the room in which it will be laid. Wood that is too dry may regain moisture from the air and swell; wood that is too wet will shrink. The acceptable moisture content is between 10 and 14% for a centrally heated house and can be measured using a moisture metre. Wood flooring can also be used with underfloor heating but in that case the moisture content must be even lower, between 6 and 8%. Because hardwood is long-lived it is worth taking care to ensure that these details are correct and that the installation is done by qualified people.

Hardwood Flooring — Our Experience

We have used hardwood only once, in a common living area, where it was going to be subject to very heavy use. We used a low-formaldehyde Scandinavian blockboard that was specially designed and laminated to be extremely stable and easy to install. There is no question that it is a wonderful material, but at nearly £40/m² it is hardly cheap. The cost is somewhat tempered because it is also a structural floor, so the labour and material for the subfloor are eliminated. It can be comparable cost-wise with a softwood subfloor and high quality all wool wall-to-wall carpet and underlay.

Hardwood flooring is a high quality material and, if you are prepared to pay for it, is well worth it.

Natural Fibre Matting — Background

Natural fibres have been used for centuries as floor covering, since long before rugs and carpets were affordable or even widely available to the general population. Even today natural fibre matting and floor coverings still provide a warm, durable, attractive and practical alternative to carpet. They are available in a wide range of colours, textures, patterns and prices. There is also a wide variety of types, all originating from plants that are abundantly renewable. Unfortunately in recent years the exploitation of these natural materials due to increased demand has led to the use in some areas of chemicals and pesticides for mass crop cultivation.

Some of the main types of natural fibre used in floor coverings are:

Sisal: from the leaves of the dark green spiky agave bushes native to Mexico.
Coir: beaten from the husks of coconuts from the tropical coconut palm.
Seagrass: from a grass grown in paddy-like fields needing a sea water flooding.
Rush: from wetland grasses or reeds from temperate areas.
Maize: woven from the maize (yellow corn) plant native to the Americas.

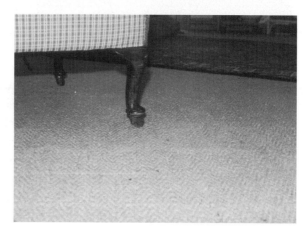

Fig 3.42
Coir matting

Natural Fibre Matting — Our Experience

We have yet to use fibre matting in any of the new houses but are planning to use sisal in the next one, a ten-person shared house, in all the bedrooms. Although some of the more exotic designs and patterns of coir and sisal can be quite expensive, they generally tend to be quite affordable at under £10/m². Maize, rush and seagrass are prone to deteriorate if they get too dry and it is recommended that they be dampened occasionally with water using a watering can or plant sprayer. One company even supplies a free watering can with every delivery as a reminder.

All natural fibre floor coverings have excellent anti-static properties and can be effective sound insulators. They tend to be tough and hard-wearing and are an excellent choice for entrance areas, where they are often seen!

Carpets — Background

As mentioned in the introduction, modern synthetic carpets can be one of the worst offenders against health in the home, providing a breeding ground for many micro-organisms, dust mites and other insects, and containing a multitude of chemicals for the prevention of mildew, mould, fungi, insects and rodents and as stain repellents. Most of the chemical outgassing occurs in the first three months after the carpet leaves the factory, which is why carpet shops can have such a peculiar odour.

Having said all that, rugs and carpets are still comfortable and attractive to most people, and there are healthy options.

The preferred choice is natural untreated wool. Wool rugs and carpets are widely available but more difficult to obtain untreated and without synthetic backing. A natural jute backing is preferable to plastic or synthetic rubber. Nylon is a fairly benign synthetic carpet material and a reasonable compromise is a wool/nylon mixture, commonly 80% wool and 20% nylon.

Rugs are preferable to wall to wall carpets because they can easily be taken up and transported for cleaning, or even just lifted out for occasional airing and/or beating. Wall to wall carpets need shampooing in place with chemical cleaners and a wet/dry hoover.

Carpets — Our Experience

We have generally used wool rugs in the main living areas but have gone to carpets in the bedrooms in many of the houses. There is something very nice about carpet in the bedroom. Because of the shoes-off policy due to the softwood floor, the carpets and rugs stay considerably cleaner than they would normally and so need less in terms of shampooing, which is good. We have been impressed with some of the natural carpets imported from Germany from Baubiologie-approved sources, untreated with jute backing. They are expensive but we have found other all wool carpets for as little as £10 per square yard. If you are prepared to pay the extra price, the all-natural option is a nice one.

Stone and Tile Floors — Background

Although ceramic clay and stone tiles are usually laid on a concrete base, they can be laid on suspended timber floor given a little extra work to provide a good structure. The basic requirement is a very stiff floor because any movement will cause the tiles or mortar/grout joints to crack. This usually means using larger joists or applying an underlay sheet intensively nailed with small ring shank nails on top of the subfloor, to eliminate any possible 'bounce' or movement.

Quarry tiles are a beautiful material, practical and durable and ideal for kitchens, hallways and entrances, conservatories and bathrooms. Used with underfloor heating they are very pleasant to walk on barefoot and provide useful thermal mass. Likewise stone tiles, although usually necessarily thicker, can make a practical, durable and attractive finish floor. It must be said that it would be rare to use stone on a suspended timber floor structure.

Tile Floors— Our Experience

We have not used tile floors in any areas except conservatories in the ecological houses we have built so far, but I have had the personal experience of doing a kitchen renovation on another Foundation house with a suspended timber floor using quarry tiles. Despite being a lot more work than anticipated, it did turn out successfully and has proved over time to hold up well.

We are in the process, as this manual goes to press, of using ceramic glazed tiles for several bathrooms. In this case we used a 19 mm plywood subfloor over which we laid another product, Fermacell, which is made from cellulose and gypsum and is very strong and impervious to water. The tiles will be laid on this very rigid surface and we are told that it is a very effective system.

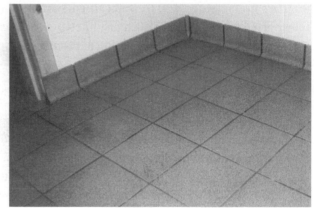

Fig 3.43
Ceramic tile floor
on timber joist construction,
Guest Lodge

Summary of floor coverings

As will be seen, there is a very large variety of 'green' floor systems and coverings to choose from. It is worth taking time to evaluate your particular needs and budget fully, because cost does vary enormously, from £5-7/m² for softwood flooring used as both the sub- and finish floor, to £50-60/m² for some hardwood floors. Even with a small budget it is possible to choose among plenty of creative and beautiful alternatives, while doing the right thing for the Earth.

Paints and Preservatives[1]

Background

One of the most important aspects of green building is the selection and use of environment- and user-friendly paints and timber preservatives. By user we mean both the person who applies the paint or preservative and the person who then lives in the house and either suffers or benefits from the products used. There are two distinct areas to define: timber preservation and surface coatings.

Preservatives: Timber preservation is a relatively new phenomenon in house construction introduced over the last few decades and promoted largely by manufacturers of chemical treatments. In the past timber would have been protected by good construction practices, appropriate detailing and paint. There are many examples of timber buildings of medieval origin, most notably the Stave churches of Norway, over 800 years old, that have survived very well despite having no chemical treatment whatever. But the modern approach is to treat almost all timber in a house, from floor joists to studs and rafters, with highly toxic chemicals, turning one of the most natural and healthiest of building materials into one of the most potentially hazardous. For it is in the timber preservative category that some of the nastiest and most toxic chemicals and compounds are found: fluoride, zinc chloride, arsenic, mercury, phenolic and chlorinous compounds like pentachlorophenol (PCP), creosote, toluene, xylene, benzene and lindane. As well as being hazardous to apply, they can continue to outgas for long periods after drying, as demonstrated by the smell of a telephone pole or power pole treated with creosote. Where there are smells there are fumes!

It is entirely possible to eliminate all chemical timber treatment by creating a well-detailed, breathing construction and using natural organic treatments for exposed wood. In areas where some form of preservation might still be considered advisable, although not necessary, as in sole and sill plates in contact with masonry, borax (containing boric salt) can be used as a non-toxic and safe alternative.

Fig 3.44
Auro Organic Paints factory,
Germany

[1] The Background for this section is based largely on several articles written by Hartwin Busch, RIBA, whom we gratefully acknowledge for his help and guidance in the selection and application of organic paints.

Surface Coatings: Virtually every surface inside the home has multiple surface coatings of oil or water-based paint, sealer, wood finish and in some places also a wood preservative. We, as occupants, are directly exposed to these. There are also various coatings applied to the exterior surfaces depending on what they are made from, i.e. timber, concrete, brick, plaster or stone. Surface treatments vary widely but ideally should be microporous or vapour-permeable (breathable) while providing the required protection for the material. As there is such great exposure to fumes from surfaces inside the house, extra care should be taken to ensure that natural and non-toxic products are used.

General Introduction to Paints and Preservatives

All paints and preservatives are dissolved or suspended in a liquid medium to allow them to be applied easily with brush, roller or spray equipment. Once on the surface, the liquid evaporates leaving the paint to protect the surface. The medium is generally a solvent, made of various organic compounds which are volatile, i.e. they evaporate at room temperature. Amazingly enough they are called volatile organic compounds or VOCs. Organically-based natural paints and finishes are substantially different from their conventional, synthetic, chemically-produced counterparts both in composition and in the way they are produced, though they both work on the same principle of evaporation of volatile solvents.

There are two types of organic solvent: synthetic and natural. Synthetic organic solvents, like white spirit and turps substitute, are derived from petrochemicals and contain other impurities taken up during the production process. They are considered by many to be the main cause of increased incidence of lung cancer in decorators. The World Health Organisation estimates this increased risk at 40%. It is a danger that is well documented and widely known about. Synthetically-based paints can also contain various mildewcides, fungicides and heavy metals which add further risk. Because of the known dangers there has been a concerted effort to reduce solvent exposure through better guidelines for safer working practices and the development of alternative products lower in solvent content.

Natural organic solvents, like pine and gum turpentine and citrus peel oil have a much lower impurity rate and no petrochemical residues and they are less harmful than synthetics. They come from sustainable sources, i.e. plant material, and generally the process of extraction and production is much simpler with a relatively low energy input. Natural organic solvents can still have an adverse effect on health if breathed in excessively, so care should be taken, as with any paint, water- or solvent-based, to ensure adequate ventilation and respiratory protection.

How the raw materials for paints and preservatives are extracted and the final products manufactured has a great impact on the environment, in terms of both the energy consumed and pollution from the chemical processes. Studies carried out in Germany indicate that the actual production and manufacture of synthetic paints creates nearly as much air pollution from VOCs as do automobiles: 55,000 tonnes per

Fig 3.45
Painting with organic
emulsion by brush,
House No. 7

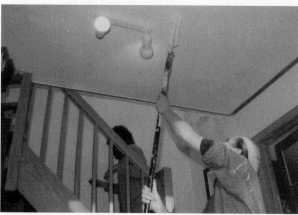

Fig 3.46
Painting with organic
emulsion by roller,
House No. 7

annum for paints and solvents vs. 65,000 tonnes for automobiles. This is not a minor offence. Organic paints also release emissions into the air, but as they come from plant sources, an equivalent amount of the polluting substance is removed from the atmosphere through continued plant cultivation and the balance is maintained. Synthetic production is almost entirely from petrochemicals and releases compounds which have been stored safely for millions of years and cannot be easily absorbed by the biosphere of the planet.

A further environmental impact results from the disposal of the material after its useful life. Unlike the ingredients of natural paint products, the compounds contained in synthetic paints, alien to those found in nature, do not readily break down or 'biodegrade' in rubbish tips and landfills, with the result that they are not easily reabsorbed into the environment. In addition a vast amount of waste is produced during the manufacture of synthetic products which must also be disposed of, and which is also largely non-biodegradable and sometimes highly toxic. This is in contrast to the lower volume of environment-friendly waste resulting from the production of natural paints, which can simply be composted.

The difference between the two approaches is obvious from looking at the main philosophy behind the production of each type of paint.

The modern chemical industry has its roots in the last century in the production and manufacture of synthetic paint and timber treatments. It is often referred to as 'hard' chemistry because of the way compounds are broken down and then reassembled into the desired product, like simple building blocks. The problem is that in each breakdown and reassembly in the chemical process there are many side products which usually become waste and must be disposed of somewhere. The more complex the product and the more processes involved, the more waste is generated. This can amount to a very significant quantity of non-degradable and sometimes toxic waste, often equalling the quantity of end product or in some cases exceeding it by as much as 30 times. As well as producing huge amounts of waste, these processes tend to be energy intensive, creating still more pollution and waste of resources.

Gentle chemistry, on the other hand — the name given to the production of natural paints and coatings — concentrates on the careful selection of raw materials to avoid processing, keeping the number of processes needed and the complexity of refining to a few simple steps. This results in both a lower volume of wastes, which in addition have a benign nature, and a low energy input.

Despite the massive waste and inefficiency of the conventional, 'hard chemistry' approach, this method of operation has become the hallmark of the petrochemical industry, which includes some of the largest and most powerful companies in the world. Like so many things in our modern industrialised society, this technology is only made 'economical' through the use of cheap fossil fuel, crude oil and gas that it took the earth millions of years to make. The vast investment in this technology, factories and equipment means that there is a certain innate resistance to any challenge to the status quo. But as concern for better environmental standards has grown, consumer pressure has caused these industries to make an effort to be greener and they now advertise more user-friendly products, such as water-based or low odour paints and treatments. On the surface this is seen to be a welcome change because of the known danger from solvents; however, the underlying processes used to produce these materials may well cause more environmental damage than the solvent-based paints they have replaced.

The trouble with water-based acrylics that are replacing the solvent-based products (alkyds) is that paint particles are not soluble in water. So in order to get those resins and binders to dissolve in water a detergent must be added; but the detergent tends

Fig 3.47
Exterior resin oil
timber treatment

to foam and form bubbles, so a defoaming agent must be included; the defoaming agents cause other problems, for example slowing the setting of the paint, which in turn need correcting, which in turn cause further problems that need further correcting down the line. All this leads to a far more complex product than the original solvent-based paint, with many more chemical processes involved which consume even more energy and produce more — and generally more toxic — waste. It is true that the end product is more user-friendly because the solvent content has been reduced, but the cost to the environment overall has actually increased! That's the aspect which is not easy for us as consumers to see.

A further difficulty arises with water-based paints and treatments when they are applied to wood surfaces. Timber contains its own inherent natural oils and resins and the best treatment will be one which has solvents able to dissolve those to some degree, allowing the applied coating to interact with the tree's oils and resins and form an in-depth chemical bond between its own paint particles and the wood. Water does not have this property and as a result bonding is weak in water-based treatments. Natural paints and finishes are based on raw materials from plants and trees, and the high quality natural organic solvents they contain do interact well with the wood's oils and resins, which results in good bonding and long-term performance.

The subject of surface coatings and preservatives is a complex one and this brief introduction to the subject cannot possibly cover more than the basic concepts and issues. It is clear to us, however, that in the context of sustainable production and safe use of these products, the only justifiable option is the natural organic-based one.

Our Experience

We have from the beginning of our project attempted to use completely non-toxic, natural, organic paint and finishes, as well as wood preservatives. The use of preservatives has been all but eliminated through the development of the 'breathing wall' construction, which because it is very vapour-permeable and provides adequate exposure of structural timbers to air movement, keeps the moisture content low enough to avoid pest and fungal attack. The construction is also well sealed and protected against water penetration with several protective layers in the roof and walls. The only area where we feel it necessary to use a preservative is on the sill plates

Fig 3.48
Group project for applying
resin oil primer to cladding

that rest on the blockwork dwarf walls, where the timber is close to the ground. We apply it really only as a precaution, using a borax-based product that is mixed with water and applied easily with a brush.

Using organic timber treatments for the exterior timber cladding, windows and trim has not always been easy. It does work out more expensive than conventional products. We found that the timber must be dressed (planed) to avoid using ungodly quantities. We had originally planned to use rough-sawn timber but found that the increased surface area absorbed far too much of the resin oil primer we chose to use. The first lot of timber had already been delivered and we were forced to do the planing ourselves on our small shop planer, which took the better part of three days.

We have since had the cladding dressed and kiln-dried by the sawmill and find the quantity of primer required is acceptable and it is easy to apply. We are using a three-coat Auro Organic Paint system, the first coat being a clear primer and the top two having an added plant-based pigment, needed to provide protection against U-V degradation. It is made primarily of linseed oil, citrus oil — a byproduct of orange juice production — and balm turpentine oil, with smaller amounts of dammar and colophonium glycerin resins, all from naturally occurring plants and trees and involving only low levels of processing. The first two coats are applied to the timber while it is on the ground and it is stacked to dry. The finish coat is then applied once the boards have been cut and placed on the house. The material is very pleasant to use and has a wonderful smell. Although the houses that have been treated with this combination have not been exposed long enough for conclusive results, we are concerned about durability, as in some places the treatment already appears to be wearing noticeably. At this point we feel we must wait and see before making a final judgment.

A variation of this exterior system is used in finishing the interior wood surfaces, with the difference that a pigment is not needed and only two coats are required. In places of high wear, like window sills and skirting boards, a liquid wax finish is used. Counter tops and tables with very heavy wear can be treated with a hard wax, as can floors. In all these applications the resin oil and wax system is absolutely brilliant to work with and is highly recommended.

We have also used organic wall paints on all interior walls with somewhat less-than-hoped-for success. Contrary to the manufacturer's claims, we have found that multiple coats are required for coverage (claimed to be one coat), that it marks easily and is less easy to clean than conventional emulsions. Overall the performance seems to be below par, though we are continuing to use it and are investigating the difficulties as well as alternatives.

Using natural paints does take some getting used to as there are differences in the flow, coverage and thinning and in cleaning brushes and tools. Some of the products require special thinners, also from natural organic sources, which are more costly than conventional thinners. Overall the organic route is more expensive, but in terms of the larger environmental picture still seems worth it. Also because we are still learning about the products and are in a remote part of the country for sales and technical reps to visit, some of our difficulties may be caused by our own unfamiliarity with the products.

We did try a water-based acrylic coating for one of the houses as an experiment before we really understood the full story behind its production. The builders all found it easy to apply with a much easier clean-up. It is too early to tell how well it will perform compared to the organic resin oil system.

It is encouraging to see that in the last few years several new suppliers of natural paints have appeared. In light of the overwhelming environmental case against synthetic paints we feel we are willing to make a commitment to stay with natural paints despite some of the teething problems we have experienced so far.

Fig 3.49 Decorating team

Section 4
ENERGY

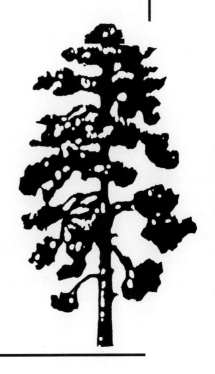

Introduction

Background

Arguably the most important environmental aspect of building when looking at the world situation is the use of energy. Currently 20% of the world's population uses 80% of the available energy and most of those 20% live in the western industrialised nations. Most of the world's pollution is caused by the consumption of that energy and the related industrial processes that have grown out of this same society. We have based our society on an artificially low and quite unreal price for energy. None of the environmental costs resulting from its use are factored in, or have even been considered until recently. Most of the energy sources we currently use, i.e. coal, oil and gas, are non-renewable and limited in supply, yet we continue to use them in ever-increasing amounts, literally as if there were no tomorrow.

There certainly have been positive benefits that have resulted for the industrialised countries, and the advances in technology of all kinds have been tremendous and to a large degree have eliminated much human suffering. But our blindness to the many side-effects caused by our consumption of energy has led us to become wasteful and careless of these valuable resources.

Clearly, if the standard of living of the rest of the world is to be brought up to that of the West, the same technologies cannot be applied without massive environmental degradation and destruction. In temperate and cold climates human beings need to have heat for their homes and a large portion of the energy consumed in our dwellings

Fig 4.1   Power station

is used to provide it. We also need energy in the home for lighting and appliances and for hot water for washing and bathing.

4.00

The answer is not to continue to build large power stations which use vast amounts of resources and create equally vast amounts of pollution and, in the case of nuclear power, highly toxic waste; or to continue to use fossil fuels at the same or increasing rates. The only long-term strategy for getting a handle on our energy consumption is to build our homes and other buildings so that they use as little energy as is necessary to provide for our basic needs. The same human intelligence that has transformed the world over the past century and developed instant worldwide communications networks, space travel and the inner workings of a nuclear power station can certainly overcome the technical problems associated with insulating buildings and using energy efficiently.

What is needed is the political will and commitment to make energy conservation a priority. Many countries have done this and have made much progress. Britain sadly lags far behind North America and many European countries but is at least beginning to look at the issue seriously. However, even the new British Building Regulation insulation standards which recently came into effect are only at the level of those of Denmark in 1935!

For this reason we have had to adopt our own standards for building insulation which are approximately 2.5 times the new standards. After several years of insulating at this level we feel we could do still do better.

Fig 4.2
The Foundation's windmill

In this section we address both the energy conservation question and the energy source issue. For along with the minimising of our need for energy we must develop clean and renewable sources to meet that need, rather than relying on the diminishing and polluting alternatives. Renewable energy and energy conservation go hand in hand.

Insulation Standards and Overall 'U-Values' in Walls, Roofs and Floors

Background

The insulation value of a building is its ability to allow or resist the passage of heat through it, known as the thermal conductance or resistance, depending on how it is measured. One is the reciprocal of the other. In Britain it is generally known as the 'U-value' or thermal conductance. In Europe insulation value is measured in conductance and referred to as the K-value, while in North America it is measured in resistance or the R-value.

Every material has a unique value for thermal conductivity inherent in its character and the insulation value varies in proportion to the thickness. Generally speaking, the more still air a material can trap in its make-up, the better it is as an insulator. The resistance of a material is found by dividing the thickness by the thermal conductivity. By adding up the resistances of the different materials that make up a wall or roof section and taking the reciprocal, we arrive at the U-value.

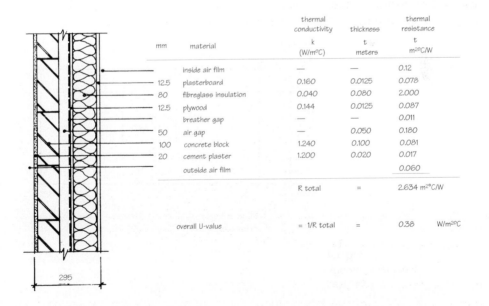

mm	material	thermal conductivity k (W/m°C)	thickness t meters	thermal resistance t m²°C/W
	inside air film	—	—	0.12
12.5	plasterboard	0.160	0.0125	0.078
80	fibreglass insulation	0.040	0.080	2.000
12.5	plywood	0.144	0.0125	0.087
	breather gap	—	—	0.011
50	air gap	—	0.050	0.180
100	concrete block	1.240	0.100	0.081
20	cement plaster	1.200	0.020	0.017
	outside air film			0.060
		R total	=	2.634 m²°C/W
	overall U-value	= 1/R total	=	0.38 W/m²°C

295

Fig 4.3   Heat loss calculations: conventional wall construction

From the point of view of wanting to conserve heat (energy), we want the building's U-value (thermal conductance) to be as low as possible.

The new British standard for roof and wall U-values is 0.45 watts per square metre per degree Celsius (W/m²°C). This simply means that for every square metre of wall area the heat lost will not be greater than 0.45 watts for each degree of temperature difference. As an example, if the outside temperature is 0°C, the inside room temperature of your house is 20°C and there is 10 m² of wall area insulated to the British standard, then the heat lost would be:

$$0.45(10)(20) = 90 \text{ watts}$$

Energy is a measure of power times time. A watt is actually a measure of power, so if you want to know how much energy will be lost through the wall then you have to know the time period. If it is one hour, then the energy lost is 90 watt-hours, or 90 watts for one hour. The common unit for energy is the kilowatt-hour (kWh), or 1000 watt-hours, which is the same as one 'unit' shown on your electricity bill.

For the above example the amount of energy lost in one hour is 90 divided by 1000 = 0.09 kWh. That may not seem like very much but if you calculate it for a 24-hour period with the same temperature difference, it becomes 2.2 kWh; over a week: 15.1 kWh; and over a month: 65 kWh. So if electricity is your method of heating and it costs 7p/unit, then every month in the cold months of the year it could cost you £4.55 just to heat that wall. In a year that might add up to £30. And that cost is for only a small section of insulated wall. There are also the other walls, the other rooms, the floor and roof, and of course all the windows and doors, which lose much more heat than does an insulated wall. If you add a double glazed 1 m² window with a U-value of 3.0 W/m²°C, then the figure for a year becomes closer to £45 — or an increase of 50% just for adding a medium-sized window!

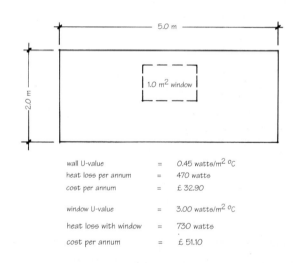

wall U-value	=	0.45 watts/m² °C
heat loss per annum	=	470 watts
cost per annum	=	£ 32.90
window U-value	=	3.00 watts/m² °C
heat loss with window	=	730 watts
cost per annum	=	£ 51.10

Fig 4.4
Heat loss through
a 10m² wall

There are many factors affecting the actual performance of a building and a full explanation is beyond the scope of this manual. There are many good books available on the subject and some titles are suggested in the References and Book List. Because there is so much variation in outside temperatures from day to day and month to month, as well as in the temperature inside a house from day to night, most heat loss analyses are done with a computer and there are many programs available. It is generally not necessary to go into a detailed heat loss analysis when good standards are used. The British government has also recently introduced The National Home Energy Rating Scheme to help owners or tenants in evaluating and improving their home's energy efficiency. The assessment is not free of charge and is intended for either existing or new homes. Details can be obtained from The National Energy Foundation, Rockingham Drive, Linford Wood, Milton Keynes MK14 6EG.

Another major factor affecting how well a building will 'hold' its heat is the rate of ventilation coming into a house, i.e. its relative tightness. Warm air holds more energy than cold air and if a house is poorly sealed around window and door frames, between floors and walls, roofs and walls, and a myriad of other places, then there can be a large loss from draughts. That loss is increased if the wind is blowing, since the increased wind pressure forces more fresh air into and warm air out of the house. The ventilation rates, measured in air changes per hour (AC/hr), can typically be 0.5-1.0 for a fairly well sealed house but as much as 3.0 or more for an older house that is not well sealed. So the amount of heat lost through conduction in the walls, floor and roof is only a part of the overall heat loss and can actually be less than the heat loss through draughts.

It should also be said that for health reasons a certain amount of ventilation is needed, to provide fresh air and to avoid a build-up of warm, moist air which can lead to condensation problems, mould and bacteria growth. In very well sealed houses of less than 0.5 AC/hr mechanical ventilation is sometimes needed. Often air-to-air heat exchangers are used so that heat can be recovered, using the warm outgoing air to heat the cold incoming air. Typically these can be 85% efficient, the main drawback being that they can break down, leaving the house without good ventilation. There is always the option of opening the windows; however this does defeat the purpose somewhat in trying to conserve energy . . . . .

The main point with ventilation is to recognise the need for some measure of control of ventilation rates. It is good to have as tight or well sealed a building as possible but with built-in devices that can be opened or closed according to need. These can include extractor fans in kitchens and bathrooms and permanent ventilators fitted to windows that slide open or shut.

Other factors affecting heat loss include: distance from neighbouring buildings, trees and vegetation; the level of exposure, i.e. on a hill or in a valley where wind speeds can be very different for the same area; gain from solar energy through windows, greenhouses and conservatories (see section on Solar Energy); the number of people living in the house or building (people give off heat!); and the personal habits of the residents, like leaving or not leaving windows and doors open, preference for warmer or colder room temperatures, how much cooking and washing is done, etc. All of these factors affect how much energy a building will use.

Being an American by upbringing but having lived in Britain for the past 12 years, I have made a personal observation that the cultural differences between people con-

Fig 4.5
Dressing for a cool
indoor climate

stitute a very big factor in the energy consumption of buildings, something which is a source of great frustration to the energy designer. No matter how energy-efficient a building is designed to be, it can be all for naught if the residents are irresponsible and/or unconscious. Americans and mainland Europeans tend to like the temperature inside their living spaces to be higher than British people do. I have decided that this could actually be a genetic trait which initially would lead one to believe that Britain has a distinct advantage over the rest of the world in achieving energy conservation targets. But the other mitigating factor is that the Brits also have a passion for fresh air, which leads them to open windows day and night, thus neutralising their initial advantage. I have not concluded this aspect of my study but personally feel more sympathy with the Swedes, who like to walk around indoors at +20°C without clothes (or very few) during their -20°C winters, in stark contrast to the stout Brits (and even stouter Scots) who prefer to leave the windows open and put on another woolly jumper.

In this section we consider only walls, roofs and floors. Windows are obviously very important as well in matters of heat loss and gain and are covered in their own section. The calculations for U-value are also somewhat simplified in that only the gross insulation is considered in the calculation, which neglects the places where studs, rafters or joists are located. The net or actual U-value will be slightly higher than that shown.

Our experience

We have aimed our insulation standard for walls, roofs and floors at 0.20 W/m²°C (R28 in ft2 -h°F/BTU) or 2.5 times the British standard at 0.45 W/m²°C (R12 in ft² - h°F/BTU). Our insulation standard is much more in line with other northern countries of similar climate. It is also relatively easy to achieve with timber frame construction, using 150 mm timber studwork, cellulose insulation and fibre boards.

Since insulation increases with thickness, the thicker the better. But wall thickness has to be balanced with other factors like cost(!), ease of construction and availability of larger timber.

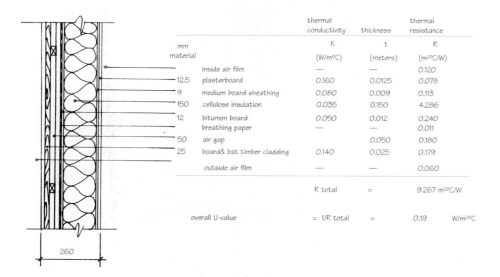

mm material		thermal conductivity K (W/m°C)	thickness t (meters)	thermal resistance R (m²°C/W)
	inside air film	—	—	0.120
12.5	plasterboard	0.160	0.0125	0.078
9	medium board sheathing	0.080	0.009	0.113
150	cellulose insulation	0.035	0.150	4.286
12	bitumen board	0.050	0.012	0.240
	breathing paper	—	—	0.011
50	air gap		0.050	0.180
25	board& bat timber cladding	0.140	0.025	0.179
	outside air film	—	—	0.060

R total = 9.267 m²°C/W

overall U-value = 1/R total = 0.19 W/m²°C

260

Fig 4.6 Heat loss calculation: our wall construction

Having had the results of a few years use of several of the houses, we have decided to increase the insulation in the roof to 200 mm (U-Value 0.15 W/m²°C = R38 in ft2 -h°F/BTU). Partly this is due to the rafter size being marginally borderline at 50 x 150 mm and 600 centres but also because the performance of the building energy-wise has not been as good as we would have liked. in the most recent house we also increased wall thickness to 200 mm and it seems to be substantially better. The exact cause of the poorer performance of the first houses is not known but it could be things like window detailing that allowed excessive draughts. There is also quite a considerable amount of moisture in new buildings that may take several years to dry out, causing a higher energy consumption.

It is also likely that it is a combination of too much window area in some of the houses and the geometry which creates large volumes and high ceilings. In most of the houses we have a very high roof space in the second floor left open to the ridge beam. A loft, used as an extra living area or for storage, is built over part of each room and is included in the heated area. Warm air will naturally rise, so the greatest temperature difference between inside and outside occurs at the top of those second floor rooms, increasing the relative heat loss. The distance from floor to ridge is as much as 4 metres. (Normal ceiling height is 2.4 metres). In balance it seems that an extra 50 mm of roof, wall and floor insulation is justified, as the price of energy will increase and the extra cost and effort needed to increase rafter sizes to 50 x 200 mm is not great.

It is important to point out that floors in a well-insulated building need to be insulated to the same standard as the other outside surfaces, although at first it may seem that, because warm air rises, floors would be cooler anyway and not need to be so well protected. Normally in a two storey house the floor would only be responsible for approximately 15% of the overall heat loss. But if the walls and ceiling have a low U-value while the floor doesn't, the relative percentages change dramatically, with

Fig 4.7
Loft in House No. 4

Fig 4.8
Winter conditions

the floor losing as much as 30-40% of the heat. In addition your feet are sensitive and a cold floor can often give the false impression of a cold room, with the result being that you turn the heat up to try to improve comfort. In a conventional radiator system all that then tends to happen is that the air higher up gets uncomfortably hot and your feet stay cold . . . and the extra energy used is actually wasted.

This also illustrates one of the arguments for using underfloor heating, where better temperature distribution and comfort levels are achieved with a relatively lower room air temperature. Because your feet are warm you feel warmer and the air temperature can actually be lower for the same comfort level, translating into a lower rate of heat loss and a saving of energy.

There are many types of construction possible for achieving a low U-value, but we have not found another that uses natural and non-toxic materials and is as economical and easy to build as ours. Most of the northern countries use a timber frame inner construction with mineral or glass fibre insulation, from 100 to 200 mm thick, with an additional foam insulation board on the outside of the sheathing. This seems the only way to get really low U-values of below 0.15 W/m²°C. Cellulose has its limits in terms of thickness, especially if the wet-blown method is used. Our experience would have the limit be somewhere near 200 mm. So, to achieve really high levels of insulation, it would seem necessary to make some compromise on the natural materials side in order to use polyurethane or other blown insulation board. In the milder northern climate of our particular area of Scotland, helped by the Gulf Stream, we probably can't justify too much more insulation, but in extreme climates like Scandinavia or Alaska that kind of compromise in order to gain extra heat retention is more sensible.

Solar Energy in Buildings

Background

Energy from the sun is the most obvious choice of a clean and renewable energy source. Solar energy is freely available all around us at most times of the year regardless of latitude, except in the very far north or south. It is abundant, free and causes no pollution or destruction of ecosystems. It is available to some degree every day, even when the sky is cloudy. The problem is that, except in sunny regions, the energy tends to be dispersed and difficult to store. So, in order to utilise solar energy for heat and hot water, we need some way of collecting it, a method for moving it to where we want to use it and a way of storing it until we do so.

Probably the best-known system is the solar hot water panel (collector). In its simplest form it is a glazed, insulated box with water-filled pipes running through it. Energy from the sun is trapped and concentrated in the box (the greenhouse principle) and the water in the pipes is heated and then pumped to an insulated tank where it is stored. It can then be used to heat the house itself or for bathing, washing or the like, when and where it is needed. This is known as active solar because it involves the use of mechanical pumps and devices that require energy to operate. The system will not work if they fail.

Passive systems can have many of the same features as active ones — like panels, piping and storage tanks — but they do not need pumps or fans, and will continue to operate without any mechanical assistance as long as the sun is shining. For example, it is possible to have a passive solar collector system like the one described above by locating the collector below the tank, and making the pipework in the form of a loop, taking care to keep the pipe runs fairly straight without awkward bends. When the sun begins to heat the water in the collector pipes it becomes less dense and begins to rise, like hot air, pushing the colder water above it around the loop. At the highest point in the system a storage tank is located. As the collector loop passes through the tank the heat is transferred to the water in the tank. The water in the loop cools as it transfers its heat and moves down the return loop to the collector where it is heated again. This is called a convective loop, because the driving force is the convective pressure of the warmer (and less dense) water as it is heated. If

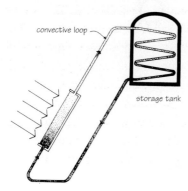

convective loop

storage tank

Fig 4.9
Passive solar
hot water system

there is not enough sunlight to heat the water in the collector, then the system stops of its own accord. As soon as there is a sufficient temperature difference between the panel and the water in the rest of the loop, the system will start to flow again. So the system is self-regulating (passive) and operates without any external (active) control.

Most solar panel systems are located on the roof where there is the best access to sunshine. Because there isn't space to locate a storage tank above the panel, pumps must be used to move the water. This is the system we have used in our houses and the type that is most commonly seen today.

Passive solar energy can also be utilised in another way, which is by designing the building so as to act like a big solar collector itself. This is normally achieved by laying the building out on an east-west axis so that the longest sides of the house are facing south and north, which gives the largest surface area access to the sun. The windows are located so that the most and largest are on the south side and the smallest and fewest on the north side (in our hemisphere; the opposite for the southern hemisphere!). This means that the south-facing windows act like the glass face of a solar panel, trapping the solar energy inside the house, while the loss through the north-facing windows, which lose energy much faster than a well insulated wall, is minimised by their small size. Finally some means of heat storage is added, such as water tanks or large masonry features, like walls or floors, located so that the sun will heat them during the day. Whatever medium is used, it must have a large capacity to store heat and then be able to release it relatively slowly. So the energy collected in the house during the day heats up the thermal store, which then gives off the heat gradually overnight when it is needed. It is also possible to have larger thermal stores that might store heat for more than a day, sometimes even large enough to save heat between seasons.

These are very simplified descriptions and there are many books available which go into the details of proper passive and active solar design. Many factors should be considered when designing a system, including the amount of solar energy available, the location and siting of the building, the amount of heat needed, the type of materials to be used, etc. This can best be done with the help of computer model-

Fig 4.10
Passive solar house
— schematic diagram

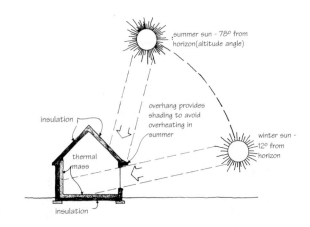

ling and experienced designers, but there are simple common sense principles that can be used that don't require this degree of sophistication and the associated design budget. It is the latter 'common sense principles' approach that we chose to use.

4.02

Passive Solar

Our Experience

Given the conditions of our site and the existing layout of caravans and planting, it was not always possible to build our houses with an east-west long-axis orientation that maximised southern exposure. In the first few houses, in fact, the gable end faced south, limiting the amount of glazing that could be used on the south wall. Despite not fully orienting the buildings to make full use of passive solar possibilities, we used common sense principles to increase what are known as 'casual' gains. In other words, there will always be some heating benefit whenever the sun shines.

In the microclimate of the Moray Firth where we are located, we have very reasonable sunshine for most of the year despite our 58-degree-north latitude. South-facing windows, double glazed without coatings or night insulation, will mean a net energy gain over a year. That means that the solar radiation gained on sunny or bright days will more than offset the heat lost at night and on dull days. By the same token, north-facing windows will be a net loss no matter what. So one basic principle is to *make the south-facing windows as large as possible and the north-facing windows as small as possible.* East and west windows are perhaps not as straightforward, because sizing of openings will depend more on inside natural lighting requirements, heat loss factors and aesthetic design considerations.

existing caravan sites

many mature trees block solar access

north

north

* houses do not have 'relationship' for good social connections

Fig 4.11　House layout for passive solar design, Bag End housing cluster

existing caravans

* buildings placed to minimise
disturbance to existing mature
trees and landscaping

4.03

north

* houses all relate to
common central green,
gable ends facing inwards

Fig 4.12   Actual site layout, Bag End housing cluster

In all of our houses we have tried to introduce the above principle of maximising the number and size of the southern windows and keeping the north-facing windows small but without compromising the need for natural light in interior spaces.

The second passive solar feature is the addition of a *glazed conservatory or sun space* on the south side. On sunny days it acts as a collector and heat collected there can be vented into the main house by opening windows or doors. When the day is too cool or not sunny enough, the openings to the inside rooms are kept closed and the conservatory space, while not generating heat, acts as a buffer between the colder outside air and the warmer living space, reducing heat loss.

Using solar energy in northern climates could be considered a non-starter with so little sun available in the winter months. But in fact solar can make a very significant impact in reducing heating requirements at key points in the year. We often have a 10-month heating season, meaning that some form of space heating is required at some time of the day or night in order to keep the living area at a reasonable temperature (16-20°C). The months of February, March, April, May, September, October and November often have a lot of sunshine and yet can be quite cold. We have also been known to need the heating on in June and August! It is at those times, the shoulder season, that the simple passive features we have incorporated can make a very significant contribution to the overall heating needs. It is true that in December and January not much can be gained from solar, with the sun at an angle of only 12° above the horizon for only a few hours of the day, and some form of backup heat-

135

Fig 4.13   Conservatory at House No. 4

ing system will always be needed. But this is not a good reason for ignoring the contribution that passive solar can make in northern latitudes.

A third feature that we have used less often is *thermal mass* in conservatories or sun spaces where heat can be absorbed during the day. Without some form of thermal store, usually masonry or water, the surplus heat generated when the sun is shining is quickly lost and then is unavailable when needed later in the evening. We have put in a masonry floor in one conservatory and are planning to build a stone floor in a living space with a large south-facing bank of windows.

These are only a few of the features possible using passive principles and we hope to be able expand the number and variety of different applications as time goes on. There are limits as to what can be achieved with solar in northern climates, but its use does reduce the overall heat load in highly insulated houses, while the addition of thermal mass for solar energy storage significantly increases the percentage contribution that solar can make.

Active Solar

Our Experience

As mentioned in Section 9.02, active solar systems involve moving parts, mechanical devices that help the system move energy and operate generally. The most common variety of active system, and the only one we use is the solar panel, the domestic hot water system previously described.

We are fortunate to have our own company that produces high-efficiency flat plate solar collectors, and naturally we have used their system for all the houses where we have installed panels. Not all the houses have them, as we have had to consider the individual occupier's budget as well. Solar panel systems range from £900 (US$1450) for a material only package including tanks, piping and controls, to £1500 (US$2400) for an installed system. This is for a normal size system of 3 or 4 square metres of solar collector needed for a typical family house. The system uses high quality materials in the panel construction: copper, aluminium, selective coatings and special glazing films of tedlar and teflon for trapping the energy in the panel, as well as the other components (valves, pumps and control equipment) and will last for a very long time with relatively little maintenance. (See Fig. 4.14)

In looking at the cost benefit and payback times, there are many factors that affect the actual savings made. In Britain at our latitude we can expect under ideal conditions to be able to collect annually about 1000 kilowatt-hours (kWh) of energy per square metre. (A kilowatt-hour = 1 unit of electricity). That means for a 4 m² system we could expect to collect up to 4000 kWh. But there are inefficiencies that make the actual amount of energy collected lower than the ideal. The collector itself is not able to collect 100% of the available solar energy; there are energy losses in the pipes; there is heat loss when the water sits in the tank and loses energy to the surroundings; and there are inefficiencies in the heat exchangers that transfer the heat between panel and tank. Finally, one of the biggest variables is the pattern of use by the building's inhabitants. In general the overall system efficiency tends to be around 40%. This may be improved by insulating tanks to a higher standard, simplifying the design of the system to avoid long lengths of pipe, etc.

We have had our panel tested at the Solar Energy Unit at Cardiff University and are told that at an 82% solar collection efficiency it is very good as far as flat plate collectors go. We would hope to get about 50% savings on hot water bills annually, giving a payback period for small domestic systems less than ten years. For larger systems, such as our 8 m² system for our Community Kitchen, which uses hot water continuously all day, the payback period will be much shorter.

We have tried to calculate the exact payback period for a given system but it is not as easy as it at first might appear. Because the savings in economic terms is important to most people, our company has developed its own 'heat meter' that actually

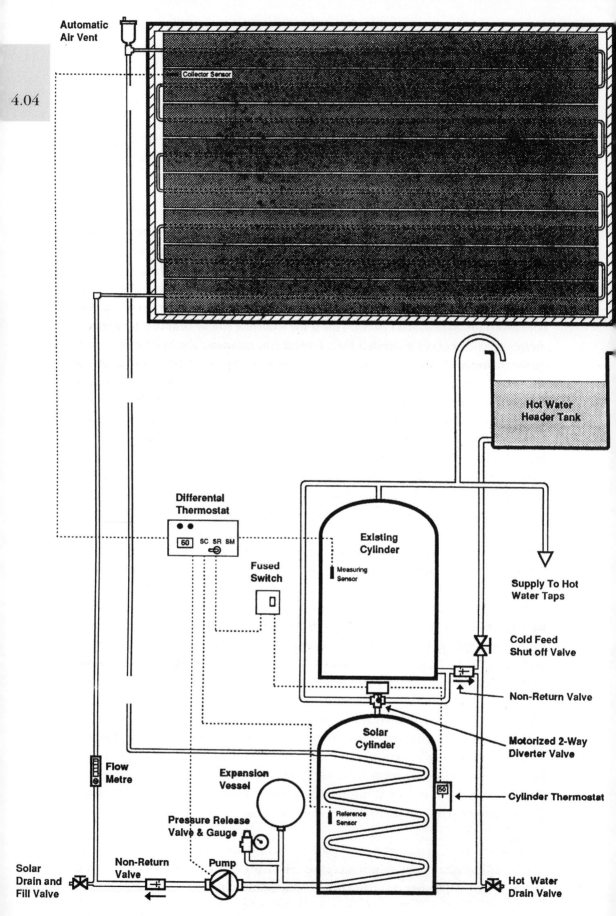

Automatic Air Vent

Collector Sensor

Hot Water Header Tank

Supply To Hot Water Taps

Differental Thermostat

60 SC SR SM

Existing Cylinder

Measuring Sensor

Fused Switch

Cold Feed Shut off Valve

Non-Return Valve

Motorized 2-Way Diverter Valve

Flow Metre

Solar Cylinder

Expansion Vessel

Reference Sensor

Cylinder Thermostat

Pressure Release Valve & Gauge

Solar Drain and Fill Valve

Non-Return Valve

Pump

Hot Water Drain Valve

Fig 4.14   Active solar hot water heating system from AES (Appropriate Energy SystemsLtd.)

measures the usable energy (in kWh) reaching your solar storage tank. In one of our high use buildings we found that the energy savings was greatly increased by increasing the tank size and insulation, giving a greater storage capacity with better stratification with less heat lost to the surroundings. This is a guest house with 12-16 people and high volume of hot water use. We increased the storage tank size to 500 litres from a more standard size of 230 litres. Since its installation in 1992, this system has been producing more than 50% of the hot water needed year round.

Actual savings made also depends on the energy source being used to heat hot water without solar. This can vary from a little more than 2.0 pence per kWh for mains gas to 8.0 pence per kWh for electricity. Obviously the payback period will be much shorter if you are replacing energy that has a high unit cost.

Another part of the difficulty of quantifying solar savings in hot water systems lies in the problem of when the 1000 kWh of energy actually arrives at the collector surface, i.e. how is the energy collected distributed throughout the year. It turns out that a large portion of this energy is available in the summer months when there are more daylight hours and the light is more intense. Because there is a limit to the amount of hot water that a family would normally use, and all of it can easily be supplied at that time of the year by solar, there are quite a few weeks during which surplus energy falling on the collector can't be used and is dissipated. The water in the tank can only get so warm, can only store so much energy, and when it reaches that

Fig 4.15
Solar panels
on a Foundation mobile home

Fig 4.16
Community Centre
8m² solar hot water system

maximum level, any extra energy available is wasted. This generally happens from the middle to the end of the afternoon, when the demand for hot water is not very great. Usually the biggest demand is in the evening and morning when people normally bathe, cook and do the washing up.

If users would be willing to change some of their habits, they could make much better use of their system and render it more cost effective. For instance, the best time to bathe is in the early afternoon, when the water in the tank is hot but there are enough sunshine hours left in the day to heat it again, so that there will be plenty of hot water for others in the evening. In fact the worst time to have a bath or shower is in the morning, after the solar-heated water has been used the previous evening or the tank has lost heat during the night. It is also sensible to do the washing on days when the sun is brightest, and generally make a schedule of activities that use hot water and carry them out in rotation during the week at the right times (midday).

As mentioned above, another improvement that can easily be made is to increase the size of the solar tank. A common error that can result in a costly missed opportunity for savings is to undersize the storage tank, which according to British Standards (BS 5918) should contain at least 80% of the daily hot water used. This is usually calculated on the basis of 30-40 litres of hot water per day per person. So a five-person house could be expected to use a minimum of 150 litres a day, and the solar storage tank should contain at least 120 litres. In some reference books it is suggested that a tank with a two-day-storage capacity is a better size. It is always best to err on the high side, because the larger the tank (and the better insulated it is) the more you will be able to take advantage of any solar energy available.

There are much better reasons than just economic ones for using solar to heart hot water, and we all know that the real cost to the planet of using non-renewable, polluting energy is much higher than market forces would reflect. If you take a long-term life cycle approach, solar will always make sense. We are completely committed to active solar. A system made of high quality materials that will operate for 30 years and more is a good investment, both in terms of the environment and of economics. Energy prices will only go up eventually, and it is only a matter of time before the real costs of pollution from conventional sources have to be included in the price to consumers. When that happens, won't those of us with solar systems already installed be pleased!

Glazing

Background

In this section we shall consider windows, doors and roof lights (skylights).

Choice of windows is a critical matter on many fronts besides that of energy. Windows bring into our living space light, warmth from the sun and a visual connection to the outer world. Good window placement and layout is crucial to the design success and occupant enjoyment of a building. Lack of adequate daylight can make rooms feel isolating and unfriendly.

Fig 4.17
Location of windows to allow maximum daylighting, House No. 4

No one can argue against the fact that we need windows. Yet from the energy point of view the best solution would be to have no windows and to use low-energy light bulbs whenever you need light! That's because energy-wise windows are extremely expensive. Single-glazed windows have a U-value of around 5.6 W/m²°C compared to the 0.45 W/m²°C British Standard for walls and the 0.2 W/m²°C that we have adopted. That means that, compared to a wall insulated to British Standards, a single-glazed window loses 12 times the amount of heat for the same area; against our wall it would lose 28 times as much.

Fortunately, we can do better than single glazing and modern windows have come a long way from the old sash types that many of us would have grown up with. Double glazing is now required in all new buildings, and with advances like selective coatings and inert-gas-filled sealed units U-values below 2.0 W/m²°C can easily be achieved. Triple and quadruple glazing is also possible and is becoming standard practice in northern countries. There are further high-tech advances that can achieve U-values of less than 1.0 W/m²°C.

The object of the exercise is to allow the greatest amount of heat and light in through the window and the least amount back out again. The greenhouse principle is based on one of the natural properties of glass, which is that it lets in the very short wavelengths of the sun's light, generated at a very high temperature, whereas it allows

Fig 4.18
Traditional sash window,
Cullerne House

much less of longer wavelength radiant heat to pass out again. Therefore when sunlight warms the objects in a house which then re-radiate this warmth, this lower-temperature heat is not so readily lost. But glass still loses a lot of heat through conduction and convection, which is why a glass greenhouse always cools down quickly in the evenings if the air temperature outside is cool.

The advance in window technology is all about improving the insulating properties of the glazing so as to capture the useful heat and keep it inside. 'Low e' glass has a special coating applied to one surface of a glazed unit that improves on the natural ability of glass to hold the inside radiant heat. 'Argon-filled' sealed units use the inert gas argon, a much better insulator than air, in the cavity between glass panes. In double and triple 'sealed units' there is a hermetic seal applied to the edging around the unit. In double and triple 'sealed units' there is a hermetic seal applied to the edging around the unit to keep unwanted moisture out to avoid the fogging effect seen when the seal breaks. The 'heat mirror' glazing system has a thin heat-reflecting film suspended between two panes of glass that is seven or eight times more effective than normal double glazing.

The drawback with high-tech solutions is that they tend to cost more. 'Low e' argon-filled sealed units can cost five times as much as standard double glazing, and 'heat mirror' even more. At these prices it would take many years to recover the extra investment. There is also the possibility that things can go wrong: for example if the seal should break the precious argon gas would escape. Still, it is generally worth some extra cost to reduce the heat loss through windows to below 2.0 $W/m^2°C$, which is the minimum standard we are working to, and there are ways to achieve it that are not prohibitively expensive. One consideration when choosing high performance windows is the amount of solar energy coming through the window as well as what might be going out. Triple glazed windows do not let as much solar energy in as double glazed units. This is because anything between 10-15% of the available energy is lost in each pane of glass, the energy either being reflected, absorbed, convected or re-radiated. In places where the maximum solar gain is desired, such as a conservatory or greenhouse, it may be better to use coated double glazed units than triple glazed.

Our Experience

We have found that the best and most advanced windows are made in Scandinavia. For roughly the same price as good quality British-made double-glazed windows with a U-value of 2.8 $W/m^2°C$ we can get triple-glazed windows with a U-value of 1.65-1.8 $W/m^2°C$ (as low as 1.35 $W/m^2°C$ with low-e coating). They come in either sealed

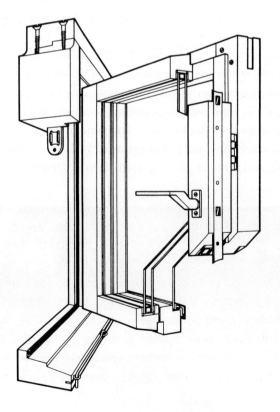

Fig 4.19
Window section,
triple-glazed double-casement
SP window,
u-value 1.65 $W/m^2°C$

Fig 4.20
Finished SP window

triple glazing or a double frame (casement) single outside pane and sealed double-glazed inside unit. The double casement version has hinges between the casements to allow for cleaning but they usually remain closed; they have the added advantage that the sealed unit, the part of the window that is susceptible to damage, is not exposed to the weather. Triple glazing has better sound insulating qualities as well, a factor that is important to us, since we are located next to an air force base.

In terms of value for money, it appears that the triple-glazed Scandinavian windows win hands down. The drawback is the order and delivery time that is involved — some 12-16 weeks or more — and the complications that any mistakes on orders can mean over long distances. It has been a continuing search to try to locate the best windows but we have always returned to our original supplier, SP-STORA.. There are other satisfactory manufacturers in Norway and Sweden but we have found none in Britain that are comparable.

It is our policy to use timber windows despite the claims of uPVC manufacturers that their windows are thermally better than wood and maintenance-free as well. Now, after twenty years of use, uPVC windows are beginning to show problems in the form of distortions, cracking of welds, discolouration and general deterioration. But the biggest problem is one of environmental pollution, as uPVC is virtually inde-structible and non-biodegradable and if burnt gives off toxic fumes. Denmark now classifies it as toxic waste.

Fig 4.21
Window installation

The type of timber used in windows is also a concern for the environmentally-conscious builder, who will want to avoid the use of tropical woods. Scandinavia has good forest management policies and the red pine normally used is a high quality timber. Properly maintained it will last for a very long time.

Roof lights

We have used Velux roof lights in all the houses to a greater or lesser degree and have as yet found no real competitor in terms of cost and quality. With most of the units we have installed we have had to compromise by using ordinary double glazing with higher U-values of around 2.8 W/m²°C. There is a high-performance glazing unit available from Velux, known as 'Veltermplus Insulation Glass', with a U-value of 1.8 W/m²°C, at about 30% extra cost.

There is not much to be said about roof lights except that they are wonderful for bringing light and a sense of space into what otherwise might have been awkward and dark roof spaces. They are far simpler and less expensive than the traditional alternative, dormers, and usually bring more direct light into a room anyway. One rule that we have not always followed is that a little roof light goes a long way and we have been known to make them too large and too numerous, which has been a contributing factor to the poorer-than-expected energy performance of some of the buildings. Too much or too many on southern roofs can lead to overheating and too many or too much on northern roofs can lead to excessive heat loss. Think of the

Fig 4.22
Velux roof light

extra heat loss factor of 14 (=2.8/0.2) that roof lights have versus insulated roofs. Despite being a virtual energy hole in the roof, though, they have to rate high in terms of human innovation, along with hot showers and the sleeping bag.

Doors

For high-performance doors, again we found that Scandinavian companies offered the best option in terms of quality, energy efficiency and cost. We initially bought from SP but because of problems with door locks and hardware have now changed to Hovland.

The main features we have looked for are good thermal insulation, as in the glazing and the core; good weather seals; high quality construction; and positive locking. One of the main problems with doors is that they warp over time and then do not shut properly, causing draughts. Most Scandinavian-produced doors latch at two or three points, most commonly at the bottom of the door, the middle and the top. That way, even if the door does warp slightly so as not to fit against the jamb by itself, the sliding pins at the top and bottom will pull it in tight. The doors generally come pre-hung and complete with frame and seals, so they need only be fitted to the rough opening.

The technology of energy-efficient doors has been well developed in Sweden and Norway and once again we have not found a comparable product in Britain.

Fig 4.23
High performance door
by Nor Dan,
Youth Building

Heating Systems

Background

In our climate we need a primary or backup heating system for our buildings despite good insulation and various solar features. We have tried to find the best combination of off-the-shelf options with as high an energy efficiency and as little resulting pollution as possible. This is certainly an area we can improve on and we have learned a lot through our mistakes.

Despite having erected a 75-kilowatt windmill that supplies 20% of our electricity and our self-imposed commitment to use as much renewable energy as possible, we are still faced with relying on some of the conventional energy fuels listed below in the short to medium term. In the long term we hope to erect more windmills and use a greater proportion of solar in our buildings. This strategy is discussed in the chapter on Renewable Energy.

One of the basic problems with the current state-of-the-art conventional heating systems is that they have mostly been designed with convenience in mind and to use the cheapest fuel possible. And with fuel oil and mains gas at quite low prices, the emphasis has not been on minimising environmental impact or on fuel conservation. There has certainly been an economic consideration, as no one likes to throw away money but, without the true cost of long-term use of fossil fuels or nuclear power being included, the cost reflected to the consumer is artificially low. In recent years, however, with more public awareness of the world environmental plight there has been more emphasis placed on energy efficiency and improvements to boilers and heating systems are gradually being introduced.

Fig 4.24
Wood pile,
seasoning timber for firewood

We shall look first at fuels, then boilers and finally types of system. Because there is a myriad of different choices and this cannot be a comprehensive discussion, we shall concentrate mainly on the options we ourselves considered and our experience with them to date.

The first questions relate to fuel. What are the choices available to us now that will meet our needs? What are the environmental consequences of using them? What are the practical advantages and disadvantages? And what are the costs involved for each?

Fuels: The Choices

The main fuels we considered were: oil, mains gas, coal, electricity, wood and propane (LPG).

Oil used in home heating is one of a number of forms of refined oil taken from crude oil deposits. Crude oil is thought to be formed from ancient deposits of decayed organic matter subjected to the pressures in the earth's crust over millions of years. It is a limited resource and the known reserves are being depleted at a rapid rate, so much so that there is thought to be less than 50 years' supply left. It is very cheap at the moment but has been and probably will continue to be highly subject to market fluctuations. It is not a clean fuel and burning it produces CO_2 and other gases, SO_x and NO_x being the biggest contributors to acid rain. Practically it is easy to use and is stored in a small tank near the house, but because it is a dirty fuel, boiler maintenance is needed more frequently than for cleaner fuels like mains gas or propane. As already mentioned, oil is not a renewable resource and is running out world-wide and is therefore not a long-term solution.

Mains gas is a relatively clean-burning fuel, although it does produce carbon dioxide (CO_2). But compared to oil for each unit of usable energy (kWh) it produces only 69% of the amount of CO_2 and 0.3% of the amount of sulphur dioxide (SO_2), one of the main contributors to acid rain. It forms naturally within the earth and is related to crude oil formation. If mains gas is available in an area, it is easy to use, easy to monitor, the supply is guaranteed and it is very cheap. Because it is cleaner-burning than most fuels, maintenance of boilers is reduced considerably. It is not a renewable resource and there is a definite limit to supply, estimated to be somewhat less than known oil reserves, so again it cannot be considered a long-term solution.

Coal as a solid fuel is perhaps the dirtiest of all possible choices, in terms both of its mining, storing and handling and of its burning. Compared to oil, house coal produces 115% of the amount of CO_2 and 223% of the amount of SO_2 for each usable kWh of energy. There are different grades available, however, and the so-called smokeless varieties are much better than ordinary house coal. Even house coal varies and a coal with a high sulphur content is the worst choice from an environmental point of view. Coal is more expensive than oil and gas but can be stored in fairly large quantities without difficulty. Heating with coal involves such a lot of work that most people would not consider it for their primary fuel. But boilers are available that can heat hot water and/or seven or eight radiators. Because coal is dirty these appliances need very regular cleaning and maintenance costs are higher. Mining of coal has its environmental disadvantages, though it may be argued that deep mining does not have much negative effect. Although the world coal supplies are large enough to supply fuel for several hundreds of years at current estimates, they are still limited, so again it is not really a solution for the long term.

Electricity is a more complicated choice to analyse because it is generated by many combinations of different power stations using a variety of fuels: coal, gas, oil, nuclear and hydro. The main argument against electricity as a primary energy source for heating is that it is inherently inefficient. Because of transmission losses and other system losses in the generation of electrical power, the useful energy obtained is only 25-30% of the potential energy of the source fuel, i.e. an efficiency of only 25-30%. When you compare that figure with modern conventional home boiler efficiencies of around 70-80% for oil and gas to as much as 95% for condensing boilers, it is clear that electricity is tremendously wasteful. There are ways to improve its efficiency but at the moment this is the situation in Britain.

With the inherent inefficiency and wastefulness in electricity production come the associated pollution problems. Compared with oil burnt in the home boiler, electricity produces 280% the amount of CO_2 and 530% the amount of SO_2 for each usable kWh of energy. This does not hold, of course, for electricity produced from clean and renewable sources like wind and water.

Of the methods currently used to make electricity, the only renewable source is hydro since it is dependent upon rain and snowfall. But even hydro has a large environmental drawback in that in order to create the reservoirs needed to power turbines, huge dams are built and large areas of land flooded. Often these are remote wilderness areas and much disruption and destruction to habitat and wildlife results. There are positive aspects to the construction of dams as well as negative, such as their role in flood control and in providing storage for a stable water supply; on the other hand only a finite number of reservoirs can be built and not every valley or glen with a potential for electricity generation should be considered as fair game by

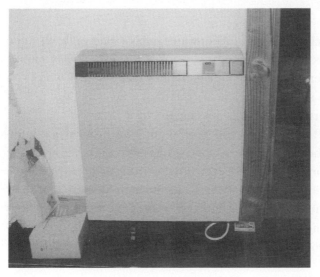

Fig 4.25
Night storage heater

the electricity industry. As with most things a balanced approach is needed. Nationally hydro contributes very little to the overall energy supply, but in our location in Scotland the proportion is approximately 40% of the total.

We shall always need electricity in our houses for our various modern appliances — radios, televisions, computers, refrigerators and lighting — so some portion of our energy bills will need to be for electricity. But the energy required for these special needs is around 20-30% of the overall consumption. Most energy is used for space heating, hot water and cooking, varying between 50 and 70% of the total. The percentages change considerably depending on the level of insulation of the house.

The electricity companies will lead you to believe that electric space heating is a good idea, and in some applications it may be. They offer special tariffs, like Economy 7 or White Metre, that give the consumer a reduced unit cost during a limited number of night time hours, with a slightly increased daily rate. By using storage heaters that heat up during the night time hours you can take advantage of the cheap-rate electricity. The electricity companies offer this cheap rate at times when most people won't be using electricity, in order to balance out the demand. Big power stations are expensive to start up and shut down and the more the daily national load is spread out the better for the electricity companies. But in our experience the reality seems to be that with storage heaters room temperatures are not easy to control and often during cold weather the heaters will have run out of heat by the time the evening comes round when it is most needed. Conversely during warmer weather they will continue to charge up at night and give off heat during the day regardless of the outside temperature, and require to be manually adjusted for each significant weather change. Because you have to adjust them the night before, you are forced to gamble on the weather change and what you are likely to need. Usually you get it wrong, just like the weatherman, in Britain's highly changeable climate. Improvements are being introduced to the various systems and it is possible that with more sophisticated control equipment it will become a better and less wasteful option. But given the general inefficiency in supply, electricity does not seem to be a good choice for heating.

Wood is another possible fuel for heating and hot water and is a renewable resource if taken from managed forests. It can be argued that wood is the best value for money as you are heated three different times for a given unit of fuel: the first when you cut it, the second when you split and stack it and the third when you burn it. This method does take extra effort, although it is possible to buy it already cut and split and pay someone to stack it! But you will still have to put it into your wood burning stove or boiler. Wood is cheap and modern wood stoves with controlled air intake and damping are efficient burners. Some are even fitted with catalytic converters to reduce smoke and air pollution. Generally, it does take the more dedicated of souls to use wood as primary fuel and, in a village context of trying to heat many dwellings in close proximity, considering the numbers of trees required each year and the resultant smoke from burning, wood does not seem to be a satisfactory solution. Where it does make sense is in remote locations where trees are abundant and neighbours are scarce, e.g. the cabin in the woods.

Propane is a manufactured gas that is widely available in bottles of different sizes. It is also available in bulk deliveries and is stored in large tanks of 1 tonne or more capacity, located near the home. **Butane** is another gas commonly sold in bottles. Both of these are what is classed as **LPG**, or liquefied petroleum gas, and are byproducts of the refining of crude oil. LPG is sold in liquid litres and is under pressure. Once pressure is reduced through a regulator it expands into its vapour form and is piped to appliances for burning. It has many of the advantages of mains gas but is more expensive, usually about double the price. It is clean-burning, similar to mains gas, has a high heat capacity and can be moved around fairly easily in its bottled form. It is used extensively in areas that are not on mains gas and where access may be limited for oil trucks. As LPG is produced during the refining process of oil, it is not a renewable energy source.

Our Experience

We started with a caravan park that was largely oil-consuming, with coal, wood and electricity used in varying amounts. Looking at the choices that are both available and practical given our resources, the best option for us is mains gas. It is the cleanest-burning and one of the cheapest of the conventional fuels, similar in price to oil. Unfortunately, we do not yet have mains gas, though it may come to Findhorn in the near future. Wood is also a good option but it would not be practical to use it for all our dwellings. We now use about 150-180 tonnes of wood per year, which is about 10% of our current energy use for the site. This is about as much as we can manage physically, given that we need a place to store, cut and season the logs before they are delivered to individual dwellings. Pollution-wise we are also at about our capacity and on a cold, still winter's day the wood smoke hanging in the air around some areas of The Park can be very unpleasant. So, even at our somewhat remote location in Findhorn, we occasionally have air pollution problems.

Our choice has been to use bottled propane in all new constructions as the cleanest-burning high heat content option. Economically we pay a penalty in choosing it

Fig 4.26
Bulk storage tank
for propane (LPG)

over oil so cannot yet afford to phase out oil altogether, with the price being less than half that of bottled gas. As we replace the very energy-inefficient caravans with our new highly insulated houses we shall automatically begin to save energy. And with higher-efficiency boilers available for gas we can reduce some of that extra cost of the raw fuel. There is also the possibility that we will get mains gas sometime in the future and the boilers and system can all be easily adapted.

The next question to consider in terms of heating is what type of boiler to use. The choice of boiler is influenced by the type of system, of which there are many. The two main types of system we look at here are both hot water or 'wet' systems: conventional wall-hung radiators and underfloor heating.

Boilers

Conventional boilers have a water jacket heat exchanger surrounding a combustion chamber where the fuel is burned. The water in the jacket heats up and is then circulated to where it is needed for space or domestic hot water heating. The flue gases, which are the combustion products of air and the fuel, are vented out through a pipe (the flue) to the outside air. There is considerable heat contained in this gas, which can be as hot as 250°C, and it is normally wasted as it sails out into the open air in a vain attempt to heat your neighbourhood. The resulting loss means that the boiler efficiency is somewhere between 60 and 77%. When modern conventional closed boilers were introduced, this efficiency figure was a great improvement over the open fires of old, which were mostly below 30% efficiency. But even at 70% there is a lot of wastage, as about a third of the cost of the fuel you are paying for goes up the chimney.

Two more advanced boilers are available now that improve on the conventional boiler efficiencies: the so-called 'high efficiency' boiler and single and double 'condensing' boilers.

High efficiency boilers use a combination of a more efficient heat exchanger (the water jacket), a higher level of insulation in the casing to reduce heat loss to the boiler room, and an inverted 'U' flue to help reduce the flue gas temperatures and stack ventilation losses. The inverted 'U' forms a natural air lock and keeps air from being drawn up the flue when the boiler is not firing, the opposite to open fires and conventional boilers. Typically these boilers can reach as much as 85% seasonal efficiency.

Condensing boilers have some of the same features as high efficiency boilers, like better casing insulation and the inverted 'U' flue. But they attempt to recover even more heat by condensing the flue gases from the combustion process. This is achieved by putting a second and sometimes third heat exchanger in the path of the flue gases. In this way the final temperature of the exit gases can be reduced to between 50 and 60°C. Typically, single condensing boilers can achieve 90% efficiency while double condensing boilers can reach as high as 98% efficiency.

The technology for condensing boilers is well developed in industrial- and commercial-sized heating systems but fairly new in the much smaller domestic-sized boiler. The effectiveness of condensing boilers turns out to be a more complex problem than it at first appears. In larger systems special controls and equipment can be added to make sure the conditions for condensing and maximum efficiency are maintained. This depends somewhat on outside temperature and humidity conditions but in the UK these conditions do exist for a large part of the heating season, usually when the outside temperature is above 5°C. The other main criterion is the 'return water' temperature and the need to ensure it is low enough to cool the flue gases below their dew point, i.e. so that they will condense. If the return water (the water coming back to the boiler after it has been circulated to radiators or hot water tanks and given up a large part of its heat) is not cool enough, then the flue gases won't condense, no extra heat can be recovered and efficiency drops. Generally, this return water temperature should be below 55°C. With larger systems the cost of extra controls can be justified, but in a domestic situation these extras can make the system overly expensive and in most cases they are not readily available anyway. So the consumer is left in a hit or miss situation, unable to evaluate how well the boiler is performing.

The other aspect of condensing boilers is that the condensate, the liquid that condenses from the flue gases in the flue, is mildly corrosive, so the components in contact with it need to be made of high quality materials like stainless steel. If they are not, then many problems will develop! This tends to make these boilers more expensive than conventional ones. There are only three manufacturers currently making

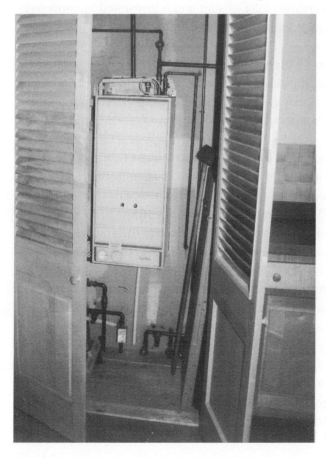

Fig 4.27
Trisave gas condensing boiler,
Guest Lodge

Fig 4.28
Plume from gas
condensing boiler

domestic-sized condensing boilers (less than 23 kW or 80,000 BTU/hr) for the UK market and they have had their growing pains in finding the best way of dealing with this particular problem.

It should be said that at present for domestic purposes condensing technology is only available for mains gas or LPG boilers. Oil burning produces a much more corrosive condensate as well as creating a lot of soot and is not suited to condensing boilers. Oil boiler efficiencies are limited to the conventional range.

Despite the potential problems with domestic-sized condensing boilers, the Building Research Establishment (BRE) still recommends their use. It will no doubt only be a matter of time before the initial teething problems are sorted out and they become the standard for gas boilers.

Our choice has been the condensing gas boiler, adapted for LPG, and despite some early difficulties with frequent boiler lock outs, which the manufacturer did correct, they are performing well. We have yet to verify the actual efficiencies at which they operate. Currently we have 7 boilers ranging in size from 10 kW to 23 kW (30,000 to 80,000 BTU/hr). These boilers need far less maintenance than oil ones, because gas is a cleaner-burning fuel, and this considerably reduces annual servicing costs.

In addition to the LPG condensing boilers we have also experimented recently with high efficiency 'combination' boilers. These are what are sometimes called a 'demand' boiler because they operate on hot water demand and do not have hot water storage tanks. They are ideal for small households with limited storage space for tanks and where a lower flow is acceptable. For example filling a bath may take ten minutes instead of four minutes because the water is heated only as it is needed. The boiler is activated by the hot water taps in the house and varies its output to match the demand in the moment. These boilers are not well suited to solar hot water systems and we have only used them when solar was not practical. The main advantage is that they do not lose energy by having a tank full of hot water in a cupboard somewhere when there is no need or demand for it.

One disadvantage in using bottled gas is that, because bottles do not hold much fuel (we use 46kg bottles), they need frequent checking and changing. We generally use a 4- or 6-bottle system with half the bottles feeding the boiler. When those bottles run out, an automatic changeover valve switches to the other half, which, if you have been vigilant, will be full. The valve indicates when the switch has been made so you can re-order but it means that you must physically check the indicator at least once a week in the heating season. If you don't, you will be very inconvenienced when your boiler suddenly stops working, which will undoubtedly be on a Sunday during a snow storm. Also, because the bottles have to be hand-connected to flexible hoses using a spanner to tighten the nut on the fitting, the possibility always exists that a leak will occur through carelessness in tightening, or through deterioration of the hoses. We have lost some fuel through leaks in these ways and so extra care must be taken when fitting bottles and hoses should be checked regularly and replaced every few years. We employ someone to make a once-a-week round to check the 30 or so bottle supplies and make our order. We have an LPG supplier who connects the bottles as well as delivers. This arrangement does work well now but mains gas with metres would, of course, be far easier to manage. Bulk LPG tanks are also available and have some of the same advantages as mains.

Type of Heating System

Once there is fuel and a boiler, there has to be a system for getting the resulting heat from the boiler to the various rooms that you want to be heated. There are many types of heating system. The two principal ones are: *wet systems* where water is heated and then pumped round the house through various objects that release heat; and *warm air systems* where the boiler heats air which is circulated through the house by means of air ducts. In Britain the most common is the wet system, and this is the type we have concentrated on, mainly because this is what is most readily available to us in terms of materials and local plumbing knowledge.

The three main wet system types are conventional wall-hung radiators, baseboard radiators and underfloor heating. Wall-hung radiators give off their heat through both convection (air warmed by contact with the radiator surface rises, creating air circulation that gradually heats the room) and radiation (the warmer surface of the radiator gives its heat to the objects and people in the room). Radiant heat is the warmth felt when sitting in front of a fire but in the case of the radiator it is much less dramatic because the radiator temperature is far lower than that of a burning fire. Baseboard radiators are located near the floor around the perimeter of a room and work by convection, heating the coolest air near the floor and creating air circulation that gradually warms the room as the heated air rises. Underfloor heating works by means of pipes embedded in the floor in which hot water is circulated. It is a true radiant heat and typically gives the best temperature profile for human comfort, with a warm floor and cooler

Fig 4.29
Typical radiator for
a pumped hot water
heating system

upper level. The opposite is the case with other systems, with the air stratifying so that it tends to be much warmer nearer the ceiling and colder at the floor.

Our Experience

We have used exclusively the conventional wall-hung radiator system, not because of any heating advantage but because it is the only system with which we are able to cope. Our plumbing expertise has been limited and because this is the system we know, this is what we have used. We have generally had our plumbing work done by a local firm, as opposed to a do-it-ourselves approach. In our first house, during the three-week self-build course that kicked off the building work, we did try to do plumbing work ourselves with a group of self-confessed non-plumbers. We then had two people work for a month fixing the 40-odd leaks that developed as a result of bad joints. When we finally gave up and called our local plumber, he fixed the remaining problems in a couple of days. We decided that he would be doing the installation work from then on and we have had no regrets.

Because of the many advantages of underfloor heating, we are seriously considering it for our next project. It does provide a better room climate; it uses less energy, because the required comfort level can be attained with a lower room temperature; and it is better suited for condensing boilers because of the lower operating temperatures of the return water. This can result in energy savings of up to 26% over conventional radiators according to studies done by the BRE. The capital costs of installation are higher but so is the expected life of the materials. With the savings in fuel consumption it would appear that this is an option worth pursuing.

Fig 4.30
Kenny Paterson,
our local plumber

Lighting

Background

Close to 10% of the energy consumed in the UK is for lighting buildings, both residential and commercial. Most residential lights are still the standard tungsten filament incandescent bulbs, more or less the same as Thomas Edison invented. They use an evacuated glass shell filled with argon to hold a filament of the metal tungsten through which a current is passed, exciting the tungsten and generating light. They should really be called heating elements rather than light bulbs, since they actually generate far more heat than light. Generally standard light bulbs convert only 10-15% of the power they consume into usable light! Usable light is measured in lumens, and the best way to rate the economy of lighting is through a measure of lumens per watt. The higher the number of lumens per watt, the more efficiently is power being used to generate light. Unfortunately this method of rating is not in general use and we are still accustomed to measuring light intensity through power consumption (i.e. in watts).

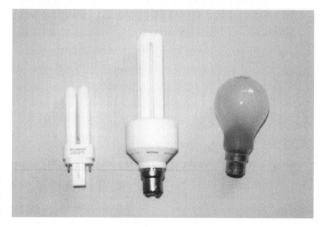

Fig 4.31
Conventional light bulb
and low energy
compact fluorescent PL bulbs

There is a new generation of low-energy lights and fixtures which can make a large improvement on energy efficiency in the home, with resulting savings to the owner as well as the environment. These are the so-called compact fluorescent lights, and they come in several different shapes and sizes. There are also various low-voltage systems available, but we will concentrate on the compact fluorescents, as they are the easiest to use, require no special wiring and fit into ordinary bayonet fittings.

At first glance it seems hardly likely that much saving can be made, since lighting constitutes such a small percentage of the energy we consume. But consider the following figures. A conventional 100-watt light bulb has a 1000-hour life and costs about 60p. A compact fluorescent bulb of equal light intensity has a normal life of over 8000 hours, but costs £15. That is where most people stop. Who can rationalise spending £15 for a light bulb even if it does last eight times as long. Buying eight conventional bulbs only costs £4.80. But investigating a bit further leads to a surprising discovery.

type		expected life (hours)	cost	energy consumption (kwh)	cost to run £	total cost
conventional bulb	– 1 No	1000	0.60		(£)	
	– 8 No	8000	4.80	800	56.00	£60.80
compact fluorescent	– 1 No	8000	15.00	160	11.20	£26.20
Net Savings over 8000 hour life						£34.60

Fig 4.32
Table of cost savings for low energy lighting

4.07

The compact fluorescent bulb is only rated at 20 watts. That means that over its 8000-hour life it will consume 160 kWh. If electricity from the grid is costing 7p per kWh, that makes a total cost for operating the light of £11.20. But a conventional 100-watt light burning over the same period of 8000 hours will use 800 kWh and cost £56.00! So if you include the bulb cost and the cost of the electricity to operate it, for every 100-watt bulb that you replace with a compact fluorescent you save £34.60.

Clearly both energy-wise and in economic terms there are very significant savings to be made, but it does require a larger initial outlay. And the 8000-hour burning life of a bulb will probably take a few years to realise depending on how much the light is used. In places where a light is used very infrequently, like lofts or storage closets, it may not make economic sense to buy the more expensive low-energy bulbs, since the real savings result from use of the light and the 80% reduction in energy consumption. The savings are also only made if the energy-saving light makes it through to its natural end, so care must be taken not to damage it so that it dies prematurely.

Fluorescent lighting has been around for a long time, and has always been more energy-efficient than incandescent bulbs. But until recently it has been available only in long tubes of 2-8 feet. These tubular fluorescents, sometimes called strip lights in Britain, have been used widely in offices and larger buildings mostly because of the energy savings. The difficulty with them has been their awkward shape and the annoying flicker that they sometimes give off due to frequency of the mains current. In the new compact fluorescents the flicker has been eliminated by the use of more sophisticated starters and ballasts and the tubes have been so reduced in size that they are only slightly larger than conventional bulbs.

Another type of bulb that is becoming more popular is the low voltage mini-spot. Used in shop windows and commercial premises for many years it is now becoming more used in homes. It has the advantage that it is also low energy as well as low voltage (12 volts instead of 115 or 230 volts). It is not as energy saving as compact fluorescents but uses typically less than half of a conventional bulb. They require a transformer, and the length of cable is limited to avoid voltage drops. They tend to be more expensive than conventional fixtures, and they give off a very nice light, better spectrum and can be used for many 'special effects'.

Our Experience

We have attempted to use compact fluorescents throughout our new buildings, more or less successfully, although several problems have arisen, the main one being to get the residents to use them. It isn't possible to use compact fluorescents with specialised lighting like normal and miniature spotlights, dimmer switches and some light fixtures. Lampshades that are meant to fit on to the light bulbs themselves obviously don't work because of the quite different shape of the fluorescents. Light dimmers simply cannot work with them. Spotlights depend on a point source of light with reflectors behind it to focus the beam, while fluorescents give off light evenly over their length, making it impossible to create the spot effect. In many areas of the houses residents have wanted to create specific effects and so have chosen not to use our wonderful low-energy bulbs.

There is no solution to the dimmer problem, but for spotlights there is a low-voltage mini-spot system that is also energy conserving. These bulbs generally have a tungsten element but with halogen added to the inert gas mixture which keeps soot from forming and lengthens the bulb life. They require special wiring and a transformer is needed for every 4-6 lights. They are also quite expensive at £50-70 for four lights with fixtures and fittings. But once installed halogen low-voltage mini-spots are 40% more efficient with double the life span of conventional light bulbs. Compact fluorescents are still the best choice, however, using only 20% of the energy of a conventional bulb. When we began the project, the range of fixtures was very small and often not obtainable in the north of Scotland. But in the intervening two years there has been progress and many more attractive and varied fittings are now available. With the increasing awareness of the real savings possible more and more people are moving to low-energy bulbs.

Another characteristic of compact fluorescents that has put some people off them is their warm-up time. When first switched on they are quite dim and take 5-7 minutes to come up to their full brightness. But this is often not appreciated since what we notice most is the brightness of the light when it comes on. Because of this some people have got the mistaken notion that they are not as bright as ordinary bulbs and have taken them out and replaced them straight away. I have found a number of these £15 light bulbs lying about in boxes for just this reason!

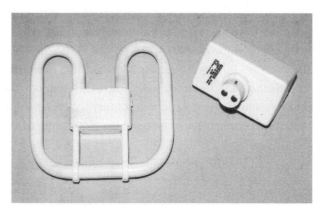

Fig 4.33
Compact fluorescent 2D bulb
with separate transformer

Compact fluorescents come in two main styles: the 2D, roughly in the form of back-to-back 'D' shapes; and the PL, with two or four long straight tubes of varying length depending on the wattage.

Both shapes come either as a single all-in-one unit with starter and ballast contained in the base, or as a two-piece unit with replaceable bulb. The two-piece units are the preferred type, since the starter and ballast will last far longer than the bulb and it is therefore cheaper and less wasteful to replace a bulb rather than the whole unit.

Another aspect of artificial lighting is the spectrum it gives off. With some of the older tubular fluorescent lights not only was the flicker annoying, but also they operated over a very limited spectrum compared to natural daylight. The best lights are those that give off a light spectrum as similar as possible to sunlight, and these are sometimes called 'full spectrum' lights.

A final comment about artificial light inside buildings is that it will never be as good as natural daylighting — the light from the sun. It is important to design buildings in such a way as to maximise natural daylighting and eliminate altogether the need for artificial light during daylight hours. This can often be achieved through the thoughtful placement of roof lights and clerestories, as well as by always locating windows on at least two sides of a roof, so that light comes in from more than one direction.

Appliances

Background

Energy-using appliances contribute something like 5% to energy consumption in the average UK home. But in addition to what they consume, energy is also required to produce the raw materials and manufacture the final product. Because the emphasis has been on convenience, until recently very little attention was given to making appliances that use energy efficiently. Consequently they vary enormously in their consumption of energy, sometimes by as much as a factor of three for similar appliances. Those that are on continuously (e.g. fridges and freezers) or used frequently (e.g. cookers, washing machines, tumble dryers, dishwashers) are the ones to check most carefully for their energy consumption.

Fig 4.34
Modern appliance store for a multitude of mod cons

Particularly important to investigate are fridges and freezers, since they can account for a large proportion of electricity consumption over the day and night, 365 days a year. In addition, they are the main culprits in CFC use in the home, not only in the refrigerant used to produce the cooling effect but also in the insulation of the shell or casing, necessary to keep the cold in. Many companies are now introducing CFC-reduced or CFC-free fridges and freezers, but this simply refers to the insulation used. Don't be fooled — there are still CFCs in the compressors!

With advances in insulation technology there are alternatives to the CFC-blown insulation and you should choose one that is CFC-free. At present there are no manufacturers marketing fridges and freezers with non-CFC refrigerants, although there is considerable research going on, as it is only a question of time before CFCs and HCFCs are completely banned. The destructive effect of these gases on the environment is well documented and there are alternatives available now, propane being the most likely replacement. Look for developments in this area and make sure you get the information on energy consumption and insulation before buying your fridge or freezer. Combination fridge-freezers tend to be more energy-efficient than separate units, requiring only one condenser and saving on materials.

Cooking also requires considerable energy. As a rule of thumb, it is best to use a gas or propane appliance rather than an electric one for the simple reason that, because of the way we produce electricity, it is less wasteful to burn gas directly. Gas hobs and ovens should, however, be provided with extractor fans either in hoods or on nearby walls to ensure air quality and avoid a build-up of combustion gas byproducts.

Washing machines, dishwashers and dryers are the other major appliances normally used in the home and again care should be taken in selecting not only the most efficient energy users but also, in the case of washers and dishwashers, the most economic in terms of water consumption. Tumble dryers are currently almost exclusively electric and great consumers of energy. Consider whether you really need one before buying, as the best ecological method of drying clothes is without doubt the clothes line. A boiler room makes an ideal drying room when it rains, so consider putting in a retractable clothes line or drying rack. If a tumble dryer is a necessity, look for the new gas-fired dryers due to come out shortly. They are already available commercially and are being developed for the domestic market now.

As for other appliances, consider carefully whether you really need them before buying. Is an electric can opener really going to contribute to your quality of life?

Fig 4.35
Freezer in boiler room,
House No. 4

Fig 4.36
Electric hob

Our Experience

We have tried to minimise the number of appliances used in the houses we have built, and to share as many of them as possible between households. One example is the installation of a common laundry in the boiler room for our district heating system. Another is a shared freezer, larger than one household would need on its own. The energy used for keeping it going serves two to three times the number of people it normally would, and the cost of extra freezers is eliminated too. The only real problem is that because of lack of space we have located the freezer in the boiler room — not a good choice in that the freezer has to work much harder in the warmer space. We hope to correct this soon!

Because we don't have mains gas on site and because of the extra cost and hassle of providing a separate bottled gas supply just for cookers, we have not used gas cookers as much as we would have liked to and have instead gone with electric ovens and hobs in most cases.

There should be much improvement in appliance efficiency as time goes on, and we intend to give this area particular attention in future additions to this book.

Wind Energy and Other Renewable Energy Sources

Background

As part of a sustainable lifestyle, we are committed to the long-term use of benign and renewable energy sources and systems. In the Moray Firth region, where the Foundation is based, wind energy combined with passive and active solar systems in new buildings form a viable energy alternative to the conventional highly polluting, inefficient and non-renewable fossil fuel and nuclear energy options.

But because of our long heating season and the intermittent nature of solar and wind energy there is still a need for a primary backup fuel, as was discussed in Section 4.06. A renewable source of energy that can be used in the backup capacity is wood. Trees for firewood that come from managed forests can be classed as a renewable energy source provided the timber is not over harvested and is on a truly sustained yield cycle. Frequently in the life of a managed forest or plantation thinning is required and young trees taken out in that process often are too small be used for construction. Burning wood in stoves and fireplaces for heat and hot water can provide the backup needed for the times when sun and wind are not available. But burning wood does produce smoke and ash, which cause problems in areas that are densely populated. Even in our remote and windy location, with many caravans equipped with wood-burning stoves we have had still days when wood smoke is a problem. Most smoke can be eliminated with better, more efficient stoves. And there is no net increase in CO_2 in the atmosphere if new trees are planted in the place of those that are cut and burnt, as the new ones will absorb an equal amount of CO_2.

Other sources of renewable energy include tidal, wave and water power. Water power in the form of hydroelectric dams and turbines, large and small, is widely used around the world. Although hydro is a renewable energy source it is not always environmentally benign and can cause massive destruction in terms of valleys and other vast areas being flooded for dam construction. On a much smaller scale, hydro

Fig 4.37
Wood stove,
Barrel House No. 5

is generally considered a good choice where there are small streams or burns with adequate fall. Wave and tidal power are still in the experimental stages and are not available commercially 'off-the-shelf'.

Our strategy has been to focus on conservation first, solar features second and wind energy third. By reducing to a minimum the energy required for a house, the proportion that can be supplied by renewables goes up. It is our belief that it is possible to achieve 60% of our overall energy from wind, 20% from solar and 20% from a combination of wood and other conventional fuels. Clearly wind has the potential for making the largest impact on reducing the reliance on fossil fuels, even in our location with an annual average wind speed of only 5.4 metres/second. This is not considered exceptional when many west coast sites in Britain exceed 8.0 m/s. The following paragraphs describe how we have begun to implement our wind power programme.

The Wind Park: The most successful system for utilising wind energy is the 'grid-connected' wind park or wind farm. It consists of a number of medium-sized electricity-producing wind turbines connected directly to the national grid. Energy is produced at precisely the voltage and frequency needed by means of an induced magnetic field inside the generator, created by mains supply. That means that the electricity produced is matched exactly to the mains and no special equipment is required to interface the two sources. Reliability of production is enhanced by the use of a number of small machines as opposed to a single large one, which was often the case in the early development of wind power. Should any one machine suffer a breakdown, energy will continue to be produced by all the others. The connection to the national grid also eliminates to some degree the need for energy storage. Early wind turbines needed batteries to store the energy, usually in 24V-DC systems. In this more advanced system, electricity can be sold back to the grid through simple metering devices when not required for owner use. The rub of this arrangement is in the need to receive an equitable buy-back price from the local electricity company. This unfortunately is not the case in Scotland, despite the fact that in England and Wales electricity can be sold to the national grid for a higher rate than it costs to purchase it.

Wind parks have been erected successfully around the world but particularly in the USA and Denmark, the latter country being the world leader in wind energy technology and production. Many wind parks are now planned and under construction in the UK as part of the Non-Fossil Fuel Obligation (NFFO), the government's programme to supply 10% of the nation's energy from wind by the year 2010.

The plan for the Findhorn Foundation's wind park consists of three wind turbines, in the range of 75kW to 225kW per machine, up to a generating capacity of around 500kW. This would produce a large proportion of our energy requirements in the range of our 60% target. We would hope to be able to absorb most of the energy directly by incorporating medium-term energy storage capability in new buildings. This storage, in the form of large capacity water tanks, combined with a micro-

Fig 4.38 Moya, the Foundation's windmill

Moya: "When the Sotho feel that something is special, they say it has moya. This translates directly as wind, air, breath, spirit, soul, or life, but what is meant is more like power or energy, similar to what the Polynesians mean by mana — a sort of force vitale."

(From *Lightning Bird* by Lyall Watson)

processor-controlled load management system, would enable us safely and efficiently to convert the energy to heat and store it whenever the wind blows. Alternatively, if the price paid by the electricity companies is close to what it costs us to purchase, we can simply sell it when we don't need it, effectively using the grid as storage. The situation now, however, is that we are paid an average of only 2p per kWh, while we have to buy at something around 7p per kWh. So we are losing 5p for every unit we sell to Hydro-Electric plc! We feel that this is extremely unfair, especially as the rate paid in England and Wales is over 10p. This is likely to change in the near future at which point it will be feasible to add more wind generators.

We completed phase one of the wind park in October 1989 with the installation of the first generator, a 75kW Vestas (Denmark) wind turbine, which we named Moya. This first phase of the project included the cabling and some of the infrastructure for future capacity. To date the wind turbine has performed well and is supplying approximately 20% of our electricity needs. This is roughly 10% of all the energy consumed on site, or around 125,000 kWh per annum.

Section 5
OTHER FEATURES

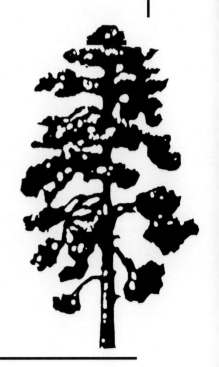

Section 5

OTHER FEATURES

Introduction

Included here are a number of other features or concepts which are important in our project and in any holistic approach to ecological building, and which deserve at least a brief mention.

Also because of the growing concern over the seriousness of the radon gas problem and the importance of eliminating it as a health risk in homes, we have included a more detailed discussion and a full description of our approach.

Services and Infrastructure

Background

No man is an island, nor is a house; and a house generally needs modern infrastructure in order to function. There are a few exceptions, like those isolated highland cottages, mountain retreats and other remote dwellings that are not provided with the modern conveniences like running water and electricity. But humans as a whole have found that when living together in communities, villages, towns and cities it is far easier to provide the basic physical necessities of living through a common infrastructure network. This generally provides clean water, waste water disposal, electricity for light and heat, telecommunications, roads, foot and bike paths, and gas or other energy sources for heating or cooking.

Infrastructure is the physical network of pipes, cables and roads that bring these essential or desirable amenities to your home. Usually they are the responsibility of the local authorities, like the water, electricity or gas boards, roads department or telephone company. Often these are government bodies but in Britain and elsewhere they can also be private companies, regulated by government authorities to ensure that they provide equal and fair services. These networks range from relatively small local systems, like water provision and sewerage facilities, that are only a few dozen square miles in area, to vast national networks like the national electricity grid or gas distribution systems which cover a large percentage of a country's land area.

Fig 5.1
Kinloss sewage works,
activated sludge method

Some of the infrastructure may also be the responsibility of the developer, particularly the network within the boundary of the development. In our case we are responsible for the electricity network, roads, street lighting, water supply and sewerage system at our site. At the moment we use the local area's facilities for water supply and treatment, but at a future time we may want to provide our own.

These larger systems have a tremendous environmental impact, particularly the treatment of waste water. It is one area that we feel we can improve on by introducing

Fig 5.2
'Living Machine'
sewage treatment system,
greenhouse interior, USA

5.10

new technology that is not chemically based, but uses natural biological and whole ecosystem processes for water purification.

Infrastructure costs are considerable and in many cases it is only feasible to use what is available, as in the case of waste water treatment now. Most developers could not possibly afford to construct a treatment facility, and so simply request a connection to the local facilities. In more isolated areas septic tanks and drain fields are used where mains sewerage is not available, although these cause pollution of ground water and are not really a good environmental choice. But until affordable ecological alternatives are available, these may be the only options.

We intend that as we develop further experience with services and infrastructure systems, in particular with sewage treatment but also with water and electricity, we shall publish additional sections for the next edition of this book under this heading.

Siting and Geopathic Stress

Background

The location, siting and orientation of houses must take into account various factors like topography, vegetation, prevailing wind direction and shelter, access, solar orientation, and location and provision of services, as well as personal likes and preferences for the site. But one factor that is not widely considered or even known about is the assessment of natural earth energies, sometimes referred to as site geobiology. There are invisible energy fields in and around the earth which can have positive or negative influences on our health and well-being. These include things like natural electromagnetic fields, presence of underground streams and watercourses, geological formations, and the composition of bedrock and underground strata.

The earth's magnetic field covers the globe in a grid of 200-mm-wide strips spaced 2 metres apart when running north-south and 2.5 metres apart when running east-west, according to a German scientist, Dr E. Hartmann. Another German scientist discovered the 'Curry grid', named after him, which runs diagonally northeast-southwest and southeast-northwest at 3.5 metres apart. Although these grids are in regular patterns, the actual magnetic field strength exhibits many localised distortions and variations. In the German-speaking countries of Europe it has been recognised for many years that there are particular areas of disturbance, notably over geological faults, fissures and underground streams, where it is unwise to build. These are called geopathic zones and are normally places where the magnetic field strength undergoes rapid change, or gradient, and where microwave and infrared emissions are also measurably increased.[1] The effect on humans is still being debated, but there are claims that in adding to an already stressed condition, geopathic stress can cause serious illness and even lead to cancer. Another German, this time a dowser, Gustav Freiherr von Pohl, published a book entitled *Earth Currents: Causative Factor of Cancer and Other Diseases,* in which cancer cases in a small village showed a high correlation to houses previously identified as being in geopathic zones.

How these zones are detected is what is perhaps the most controversial aspect, as it generally involves the use of dowsing, a practice that the traditional scientist does not usually appreciate. But the art of dowsing is an ancient one that does seem to work, with the dowser able to use a simple device like the dowsing rod and his own body to sense various energy fields. When we had a problem with our sewer at an older property we have in Forres, we discovered that most water authorities and other underground services companies employ professional dowsers to help them locate pipes and cables. Because of the age of this particular property there was no record or map of where the sewer ran and when we found that it was backing up

---

[1] *Caduceus,* Issue 7, 1989: 'Are You Building in a Safe Place?' by Rodney Girdlestone.

Fig 5.3
Dowsing

5.21

we could not trace where the problem was. After many days of trying to discover the route of the sewer by all the logical methods, the water board brought out their secret weapon, a dowser, who with his dowsing rods found in less than an hour not only the location of the line but also the precise place where it had ruptured.

Our Experience

We did have all our sites dowsed by various people and were satisfied that there was no particular geopathic stress danger.

There are remedies for houses that are located in a geopathic zone. They vary from buying an electrical device that apparently neutralises harmful earth energies, to the use of shielding under-blanket, to the insertion of metal rods and bars in key places to divert the field away from the house or bedroom.

We cannot endorse any of these methods as proven, but only say that for many they have apparently been helpful, while many other people remain sceptical. We leave it to individuals to experiment for themselves. There are certainly many mysteries of the earth and its systems that we do not yet understand, and this may well be one of them.

Radon Protection

Background

Radon is a radioactive gas produced from the decay of naturally occurring uranium which is or can be present in small amounts in the soil, bedrock and groundwater. Radon is odourless, colourless and tasteless but is by far the most dangerous air pollutant if allowed into the home. It can be found in most areas of the UK but its concentration is low relative to the rest of Europe. There are, however, particular 'hot spots' that have quite high concentrations.

The main risk is not from radon itself but from the products of radon decay, called 'the daughters of radon' (I am not making this up!). These are inhaled directly or become attached to airborne particles that are breathed into the lungs. As radioactive decay occurs they emit damaging radiation that can seriously degrade the lung tissue. From studies carried out in America it is estimated that up to 20,000 lung cancer deaths per year in the US are caused by exposure to radon, making it the second largest cause of the disease after cigarette smoking. In the UK the National Radiological Protection Board (NRPB) estimates that 2,500 deaths per year from lung cancer can be attributed to radon exposure.

Radon generally enters the house through cracks in the foundations and floor slab, and gaps around service pipes, drains and cables. It can also be given off from: household water if it comes from wells in geological formations that are prone to radon; interior building materials like concrete, blockwork, gypsum plaster and plasterboard; and even stoneware pottery if the raw materials contain trace amounts of uranium.

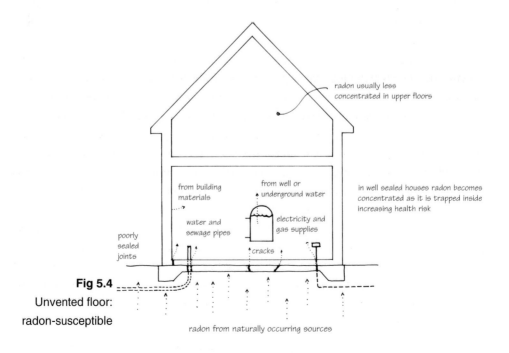

radon usually less concentrated in upper floors

in well sealed houses radon becomes concentrated as it is trapped inside increasing health risk

from building materials

from well or underground water

water and sewage pipes

electricity and gas supplies

poorly sealed joints

cracks

Fig 5.4
Unvented floor:
radon-susceptible

radon from naturally occurring sources

There is no way of predicting the level of radon in a house, whether in a high or low risk area, as the variance can be great even between adjacent houses. Houses with basements are more prone to problems than those without, as radon will collect at the lowest point, averaging 2.5 times higher than in the rest of the house. Energy-efficient, tightly sealed homes — if not detailed properly for radon control — generally have a much higher concentration of radon than poorly sealed homes. The higher you go in a house the less the concentration is likely to be.

The good news is that radon testing is easy to do and is the only way of really finding out whether there is a potential radon problem in your house. Radon is measured in Becquerels per cubic metre (Bq/m³), which represents the radioactive decay of one radon atom per cubic metre of air per second. The average value for the UK is 20 Bq/m³ but this is a population-weighted figure, including people living in multistorey dwellings where the concentrations are very low. A more realistic figure for ground floor concentrations in UK homes is around 50 Bq/m³. The NRPB has recently set the action level — the level at which remedial action should be taken — at 200 Bq/m³. The previous value was 400 Bq/m³.

There is controversy over what is an acceptable level of radon exposure, as the health effects of long-term low-level exposure are unknown. The American Society of Heating, Refrigeration and Air-Conditioning Engineers (ASHRAE), a well-respected body that sets standards for indoor air quality in the US, has recommended an action level of 73 Bq/m³. It is worth thinking about the fact that this figure represents the radiation equivalent of approximately 100 chest X-rays per year!! It is highly likely that, as time goes on, the level of exposure that is considered safe will continue to go down.

The good news is that there are a number of simple measures which may be taken to reduce the radon level in existing homes; and that for newly built homes, detailing to avoid radon problems is easy and effective.

Our Experience

We have chosen the most widely recommended option for our new homes, that of a suspended floor with underfloor ventilation. Radon is easily dispersed by good ventilation, and there is no better way than by allowing a free flow of outside air at the main entry point for radon into the building. There are other sources of radon, when it is contained in ground water or in the materials used to build the house, but these are more minor. If they are significant, they will show up in the simple tests available to check radon levels.

When we ran tests for radon in a conventional building on our site, built on a poured concrete slab, we measured 45 Bq/m³ (in our Universal Hall building). We also recently carried out a six-month test on the ground floor of one of our new houses and measured only 12 Bq/m³. The two tests confirm that we are in an area where radon is present and that the construction we are using does have the desired effect of reducing the radon levels.

The avoidance of a concrete slab does mean that the foundations are more complicated and slightly more difficult to build. But the reduction in radon risk seems worth the extra trouble. It also means that we can incorporate a 'breathing floor' into the construction for higher insulation levels and added breathability of the building fabric.

There are detailing methods to avoid radon build-up that can be used with slab foundation construction, so it does not mean that you can't use this type of construction. It involves taking more care in providing an effective barrier, either through the use of special membranes or by providing ventilation under the slab through gravel beds with perforated pipes and mechanical fans to draw the radon away from the house. There are a number of specialist firms that can provide complete details for specific applications.

But prior to that, whether you are investigating an existing house or thinking of building a new one, it is best to find out if you are in a particularly radon-prone area, or one of the so-called hot spots. The very simple tests that you can do yourself and then send away for analysis are available in the UK from Track Analysis Systems Limited, H.H. Wills Physics Laboratory, Tyndall Avenue, Bristol BS8 1TL, Tel. 01272-260353. Because the problem is now quite well known, other countries will have similar services available. Information is usually available through the local government environmental agency.

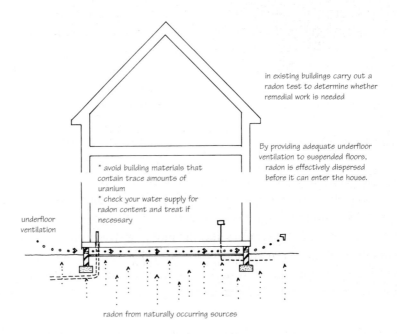

in existing buildings carry out a radon test to determine whether remedial work is needed

By providing adequate underfloor ventilation to suspended floors, radon is effectively dispersed before it can enter the house.

* avoid building materials that contain trace amounts of uranium
* check your water supply for radon content and treat if necessary

underfloor ventilation

radon from naturally occurring sources

Fig 5.5   Vented suspended floor: prevents radon build-up

Water Conservation

Introduction

Every house needs a water supply, even if it is the hand pump outside by the well or the running stream in the back garden. In Britain we generally have a good water distribution system with adequate rainfall and water reserves to provide for our needs. But there is a growing crisis over the quality of fresh, pure water with the assault by our modern lifestyle and the ever-greater levels of pollution found in tap water. Worldwide we are experiencing increasing droughts and a lowering of the water table. Water has usually been taken for granted here in our wet maritime climate, and the motivation for conserving it has been largely absent. It is only in recent years that public attention has been focused on the problem by the droughts in the south of the UK, and we have realised that clean water is not something to be taken for granted or wasted needlessly.

Fig 5.6
The Findhorn River

Because there has not been the awareness or incentive to conserve water, many of our collective practices are wasteful. Often we are even encouraged in our waste-fulness by products and appliances that use far more than is needed. As a result there are many areas in the house where simple water conservation principles can be applied.

Household Use: In the UK the approximate average consumption of water is 130 litres per person per day. Household domestic water use is broken down in approximately the following way:

Toilets	35-45%	Drinking/cooking	5-10%	Dishwashing	5%
Showers/Baths	20-30%	Laundry	8%	Garden/car	2%

Looking at this breakdown it is easy to see where the most savings can be made. Toilets are notorious for their over-consumption of water. Many older toilets use as much as 20 litres per flush, while newer water conservation models get by with under 5 litres. Baths can consume 100 litres of water or more, while it is possible to have a good shower using 30 litres. Dishwashing and clothes washing machines can vary enormously in their water (and energy) consumption, some machines using two or three times as much as others to perform the same work. And with flow restrictors and/or self-closing taps installed in sinks and basins, consumption can be cut down even further.

The other consideration in looking at water consumption is that very little of the water we use needs to be of drinking quality standard. It is one of the craziest and most wasteful of all our modern practices that we spend vast amounts of money and resources in collecting, storing, treating and then transporting beautifully clean water through complicated underground pipe networks direct to our homes, only to use nearly half of it for urinating and defecating in. We then have to spend more money and resources carrying that fouled water away and trying to make it clean again, but never quite succeeding. There is a real case to be made for not using water at all, but various forms of dry, composting toilets instead. There is technology available for dry toilets, but it is not widely accepted and in our opinion still needs further development before it will be. In the meantime we could use greywater (see below), or rainwater, for our toilets. That alone would cut our water consumption almost in half.

Clearly in designing new dwelling houses priority needs to be given to minimising water consumption through careful assessment and selection of fittings, fixtures and appliances that use less water. Because of the wide range of water consumption levels it is important to find out from manufacturers the relevant water use rates.

Minimising consumption also reduces the amount of waste water that needs subsequent treatment, which is a growing problem even in the most advanced industrialised nations. It must be stressed that our existing sewage treatment facilities are not coping well due to the imperfect chemical/biological purification processes in use, increased flow and undersizing of works. There is still a very significant proportion of sewage that is discharged untreated into rivers and seas, the 'long outflow pipe' being just another way of avoiding the problem altogether. "Dilution is no longer the solution to pollution," as one expert has put it.

Fig 5.7
Ifö low-flush toilet
(3.5 litre/flush)

Fig 5.8
Shower/bath

Our Experience

Up to the present we have not been able to implement as many water conservation features as we would like. Our main efforts have been in installing low-flush toilets which use 3.5 litres per flush, easily the lowest of any flush toilet available today. They are a high quality Swedish-made model, equal in every way to conventional toilets. And they work. Compared to the 9-15 litres that new toilets use they are a very easy way of saving significantly without any effort.

The second conservation measure we have implemented is to provide showers rather than baths in every house. Not everyone will be satisfied with living without the occasional hot soak, and we have usually put in one tub per house, making sure that it was a shower/bath so that it can also be used as a shower only. In our more intensively used houses for short-term visitors we have not installed baths at all, rationalising that most people can live without them for a little while at least.

We have also looked at various devices for regulating water flow, like flow restrictors and self-closing taps, so that water will not be wasted if taps are left open and so that excess pressure will be reduced to avoid unnecessarily high flow rates. Unfortunately we have not found any really suitable products that we can wholeheartedly recommend, although we are continuing to investigate. But even with these two simple measures we expect to reduce our water consumption by somewhere around 35%.

Waste Water Treatment

There are basically two different types of waste water that flow out of our homes and need treatment: 'greywater' and foul or 'blackwater'. Blackwater is from toilets and more highly polluted sources like kitchen sinks and dishwashers, where dirt, grease and detergents are heaviest. Because blackwater contains harmful and toxic pathogens from human excrement, it must be handled carefully and requires thorough treatment before being discharged into waterways or soakaways in the ground.

Greywater is only mildly polluted and comes from the rest of the household uses, like showers, baths and hand basins. Because it is less polluted it requires less treatment, which can be done on site, after which it can be reused. One difficulty with modern waste water systems is that there is no distinction made between these two quite different streams, and they are mixed together in the same discharge pipe. All the water must then be treated to the highest standard, costing far more than it need do.

Our Experience

We started out with the idea that we would separate the two streams of waste water and installed two sets of drain pipes, connecting toilets and kitchen sinks to one and all other water-using fixtures to the other. It was only when we tried to find a suitable greywater treatment system that we realised this is still rather experimental and not fully tested. At the same time we discovered that the foul water treatment system we hope to use in future requires a minimum flow to function properly that would not be met without the addition of the greywater flow. Partly this is due to the reduced flow that results from the conservation measures we have introduced — a sort of catch 22. In the end we joined the pipes outside the house and stayed with the one-flow system.

The treatment system we intend to use is known as Living Machines and was first developed in America by John Todd of Ocean Arks International and founder of the New Alchemy Institute. It uses a miniature marsh and aerated lagoons contained within a greenhouse. The driving power is the entrapped sunlight which gives energy to the micro-organisms, plants and fish living in clear-walled solar tanks. Within each section of the waste stream flow, the various plants and bacteria establish themselves, breaking down and feeding on the different nutrients in the waste stream. Our pollutants are food to other life forms! The result is a very high degree of water purity and a system that is robust and versatile. It is based on a whole ecosystem approach that replicates nature's own processes, which it intensifies while requiring less land area because of the use of the greenhouse.

The first UK Living Machine is currently under construction here and promises to offer a rich testing ground for natural sewage treatment in Europe. Details will be available on request.

Fig 5.9
Living Machine
greenhouse

Recycling of Rainwater

Malcolm Wells, one of foremost advocates of earth-sheltered architecture, describes in his book *Gentle Architecture* how, while visiting the New York World's Fair in 1964 and admiring the marvels of modern architecture, he had the sudden realisation of the vast waste of rainwater that results from modern building design, depriving the earth of that valuable and essential nutrient. Buildings occupy land that would otherwise support life and absorb the rains that fall on it. The sterile materials of our modern buildings shed the rainwater and divert it away from the earth it came to nourish. On reflection Wells calculated that up to that point in his life as an architect, the buildings he had been responsible for designing had repelled some 500 million gallons of rainwater, 'water that should have fallen toward what should have been soft, moist, living earth — and a season of usefulness'. Instead it was put into pipes and drainage ditches, and eventually into streams, rivers and the sea, denied its natural path through the earth and the aquifers that allow it to offer its life-giving qualities to the land.

Rain, literally the water of life, is one of our most precious resources and we do need to think about the consequences of our collective actions when we cover the earth with buildings. The land area of Los Angeles is 70% concrete and asphalt. No one really knows the effects of such an obviously unnatural condition on the microclimate and inhabitants. Malcolm Wells's solution was to begin to build earth-covered houses so that the rain still could feed the living earth, which was only slightly displaced by the buildings underneath it. We also have tried this technique, fairly successfully, but it is not always possible to use turf as a roofing material. Collecting rainwater and using it productively is the next best thing.

Collecting rainwater for use in gardens is simple and easy, though the type of roof and flashing as well as local air pollution conditions need to be considered. Houses with lead flashings are not suitable because the lead is gradually leached into the water, a process that can be exacerbated by acid rain, and in turn builds up in the soil and any plants grown in it .

Our Experience

Rain butts, large 150-200-litre barrels made from plastic or wood, are the normal method for collecting rain water. They are placed under downpipes and fitted with a hose tap slightly above the bottom. Ideally they are elevated by half a metre or more to give better pressure for watering.

Fig 5.10
Rain butt for collecting
rainwater, made
from a re-cycled whisky cask

185

Most garden supply centres have various-sized rain butts, mostly plastic. But being reluctant to use plastic we found a source of old wooden whisky barrels of around 150 litres' capacity and converted them to water barrels. When the barrels are full an overflow pipe takes the surplus into a soakaway, where it can follow its natural path, only slightly diverted by the house itself. A soakaway is simple to construct, generally being a lined pit filled with hardcore and gravel that allows the water literally to soak away. It needs to be lined to prevent the surrounding soil from being pulled into the stones and increasing the time needed for the water to drain.

We went to considerable effort to flash the roofs in copper to avoid the lead problem, as copper is much more stable and less likely to dissolve. It would be our intention in the future to experiment with using rainwater for toilets and other functions not requiring drinking quality water. This will mean some minimal filtering and possible treatment, with the design of a clever system for pumping the water to a storage vessel or WC .

Electrical System and Electrostress

Background

Electricity in the household is a relatively new phenomenon given that it has only been in the last few decades that most houses in the western world have had mains supply. But since its advent the rapid developments in electrical technology, energy, information systems and the overall electronics boom have made it unthinkable to most people to consider living without it. What is perhaps not widely appreciated about electricity is that there are subtle and invisible fields associated with it. Because of the electric charge between the live and neutral cables, a static electric field carrying an electrical potential (voltage difference) will surround an electric cable or appliance even when it is not in use. As soon as current begins to flow a magnetic field is generated, the so-called electromagnetic field (EMF) made use of in electric motors, solenoids and many other devices.

As a result of not having considered these invisible effects, we now live amid an amazing array of artificial (i.e. not part of the natural environment) electric and electromagnetic fields that are given off by our new technological toys. The effect of these on us as humans is not fully understood but the evidence is growing that their presence is not neutral and can lead to 'electrostress', manifesting in symptoms like high blood pressure, disturbed sleep, increased allergy sensitivity, headaches and nausea. Of particular concern are the extreme low frequency (ELF) electromagnetic fields created by mains electricity, defined as in the range of 1-100 hertz (Hz = cycles per second). This happens to be the same frequency range as that of the human brain, which emits waves from 1 Hz while we are sleeping to 10 Hz when we are awake, reaching as high as 20 Hz when we are excited.

This is coincidentally (or not) also the same frequency as the pulsating magnetic wave pattern on the earth discovered by Prof. W. O. Schumann in 1952, now called 'Schumann Waves', which also fluctuates between 1 and 20 Hz. Given that human beings have evolved within this field perhaps it is not surprising that when deprived of this natural context, as is the case in high flying aircraft where the strength of the field is weak, people suffer disorientation and distress as the biological clock is disrupted. The effect is more dramatic in space travel where the Schumann Wave field is completely absent. The early astronauts suffered exhaustion and extreme distress until Schumann Wave simulators were installed in their spacecraft to provide that natural pulse at 7.83 Hz. It is now a standard feature on all NASA space flights.

Modern mains electricity supply in the form of an alternating current, which moves between a positive and negative charge at a relatively constant voltage, is very different from the earth's natural field. It is this rapidly alternating current (AC) which

Fig 5.11
Mains alternating current (AC)
and frequency at 50 Hz

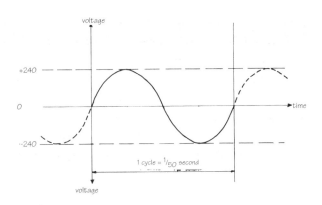

is thought to be harmful, as fields created by direct current are much more akin to the naturally occurring fields of the earth and our bodies. In North America electricity is supplied at 120 volts and 60 hertz, while in UK and Europe it is 240-220 volts respectively at 50 hertz. Cables run in the walls, floors and ceilings to supply socket outlets, lights, switches and appliances. The fields associated with appliances and cables are not blocked by ordinary walls and building fabric, and you may find yourself sitting in a strong electrical field given off by an appliance in the next room or from cables in the wall. Light fixtures in the ceiling of a ground floor room affect the room above, which will often be a bedroom.

The strength of these fields is measured in volt/metre (V/m) and is a function of the power use or current flow and the distance from the source. So things like electric blankets that are immediately next to us tend to have a greater effect than say a light fixture across the room. To give some idea of relative values, an electric blanket field has a strength of around 250 V/m, while a food mixer is around 50 V/m. Electromagnetic fields from high voltage overhead transmission lines are in the region of 2500 V/m at 125 feet and are known to be hazardous to residents living in dwellings directly underneath them.

The body operates as a complex bioelectric, biochemical organism, with cells and particles carrying weak electric charges from the brain and other areas through neural circuits. By contrast with human-created electric fields the electrical potential in human bodies is in the range of 40 microvolts. Recent research suggests that the human body is also affected by electromagnetic propagation from the brain, the way

Fig 5.12
High tension electricity pylon

radio waves are sent to operate your radio receiver and amplifier and produce music. The order of magnitude difference in the power between artificial (110-240 volts) and body systems (40 microvolts) is huge, and it seems unlikely that the larger artificial field does not in some way affect or interact with the weaker body field. Birds and other animals are sensitive enough to the earth's natural EMF that they use it for navigation. It makes sense that EMFs which overlap and interact with our bioelectric field, and which animals are sensitive to, will affect us, just as a secondary magnetic field affects the functioning of a compass orienting to the earth's magnetic field.

In addition to the invisible fields given off by electric cables, appliances, lights and heaters there are other dubious effects. Some electrical devices like televisions and computers give off static electricity and at the same time deplete the negative ions in the air. Static electricity can accumulate in the house and add to the build-up of electric fields on metal objects, like radiators, pipes and bedsprings, which can themselves be magnetised and create a strong field.

All these combined influences created by artificial or man-made EMFs and exacerbated by static electricity and lack of negative ions in the air lead to some very alien and unnatural conditions in which we spend our indoor lives.

It must also be said that research into electrostress is only embryonic and much more will need to be done before we know the true effects of exposure to electricity. Following the philosophy of Baubiologie that we should endeavour to replicate the stress-free natural environment, it seems a safe bet to try and minimise these fields. As EMFs are measurable, it is easy to check your house for the strength of fields and to reduce them through rewiring or the use of other devices. Of course, the simplest way would be simply to switch off the mains!

It should also be said that although there may be dangers associated with EMFs in the home, it is not a good idea to become overly worried about them and add to the stress level. Instead take steps to learn more about the problem and determine whether you want to try to alter your particular situation. For instance you might try experimenting yourself to see whether you notice a difference in your energy by not sleeping under an electric blanket or by unplugging all the electrical appliances near your bed.

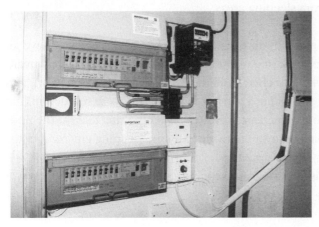

Fig 5.13

Typical consumer unit circuit breakers and distribution box.

Fig 5.14

Overloaded socket in bedroom

5.24

The most important area to monitor is the bedroom, since this the place where we generally spend the largest portion of our time and where during sleep the need for rest is greatest. There are several ways to do it: by manually switching off electricity before bed at the mains; by installing automatic circuit breakers that operate on a demand basis, switching off the electricity automatically when none is called for; or by the use of shielded cables that effectively block EMFs.

Our Experience

We investigated shielded cables, since this in some ways would be the easiest option, requiring no other particular change than simply replacing conventional wiring. But at the time of our first project we actually could not find a commercially available cable that would properly shield EMFs. Other specialist cable for internal wiring is vastly expensive and it is unlikely that any economic alternative can be found.

We opted for demand switches, connected at the fuse board where a 4-volt DC circuit is used to sense when power is demanded. When there is no demand, electricity supply to the cable is switched off, eliminating all static electrical fields and EMFs. This means that before retiring at night you need only make sure all appliances are switched off or unplugged and lights turned off. If you do require a light in the middle of the night, it will still come on immediately at the flick of the light switch. It does require some careful planning so that appliances like boilers, controls, fridges and freezers that need a continuous supply have separate circuits and the wiring to them is located well away from sleeping areas.

We failed to do the careful planning in the earlier houses and as a result have an imperfect application. We installed ring mains covering several rooms which meant that sometimes it is not possible to check whether everything is switched off, and in one case we did not give the fridge a separate circuit. We were rescued in that case by the use of sleeping lofts which are well away from the ring main at the floor level and so most residents still enjoy a relatively EMF-free sleeping environment.

In the next houses we are installing separate spur circuits for bedrooms which will be more easily controlled by the occupant.

We have also recently become aware of the availability of chlorine-free electric cables for internal wiring. Ordinary pvc twin and earth cable, used for most wiring in the home, does outgas various chemicals and in the event of fire gives off highly toxic chlorine fumes. So far we have not had the opportunity to use the chlorine-free cables.

Fig 5.15

Alain Barrère — community electrician

Shared Facilities

Background

In the suburban single-family detached-house model of much of the western world there is a sense of freedom, convenience and affluence, but also there is tremendous duplication and waste. Each household is equipped with its own personal set of appliances, amenities and features that in America would constitute what is known as the 'American dream' and is increasingly the British dream as well: the large and well equipped kitchen with microwave, toaster, refrigerator, freezer, food processor and cooker; the laundry with automatic washer and tumble dryer; the garden shed with all the typical garden power tools; home entertainment centres with stereos, videos and television; the two-car garage; and the home workshops for woodworking, sewing, crafts and hobbies.

There is no question that we would consider many of our modern conveniences essential for modern life. The independence and freedom they convey make a positive contribution to our physical and emotional well-being. On the other hand, in themselves these conveniences do not hold the secret key to our happiness, and being so self-contained, having all that we require within our own home, can cause us to become isolated and disconnected from our neighbours. The extra energy and resources that are needed to process the raw materials and produce the goods do exact a cost from our environment. It is possible to share with others many, though not all, of our modern amenities and save considerably on the resources and money needed to make them, while deriving the added social benefit of more contact and cooperation.

Co-Housing: One of the fastest-growing housing movements in Europe and America is the alternative to suburbia called co-housing. Groups of families and individuals gather together and build small developments for from 30 to 100+ people. The essential feature is sharing — both the physical amenities and socially. Each family, individual or group of individuals living together has their own living space or house with the basic requirements for self-contained living. The communal facilities available to all include things like a large kitchen and dining area for eating together, par-

Fig 5.16
Community Centre
dining room

Fig 5.17
Community Centre kitchen

ties and meetings; laundry facilities; a common lounge; sports facilities; workout rooms; workshops; common gardens and allotments; child care facilities; larger appliances like freezers; and much more.

Some co-housing groups eat together every day, with the cooking shared between the adults on a rota basis; others eat together maybe only once or twice a month. Some groups have built a single building or several large buildings where each living group has its own flat, with the shared areas and facilities in the same structure; others have detached or semi-detached houses grouped in small clusters that share a larger communal building.

The specific forms are quite varied amongst the hundreds of co-housing groups that now exist, but the main principles are the same. Sharing with others in larger extended-family-sized groups, much larger than the nuclear family but smaller than a village or town, is a rich and rewarding experience both socially and physically. It is not a 'commune' where everything is shared. Each living group — be it a family with children, a couple, a single person, a small group of adults, single parents with children — has its own private space, which gives its members the freedom to choose how much they want to interact. We all have different needs for privacy or togetherness at different times in life, and the co-housing model seems to work very well for many people in balancing and fulfilling these changing needs.

Our Experience

The Foundation is in some ways already a co-housing living group, with some differences. Most people living in The Park also work here and the number of people is in excess of 200, which makes it larger than most co-housing groups. But we do have a communal kitchen that cooks lunch for many of the residents, a dining area, large and small meeting spaces, a laundry and other facilities. What that has allowed us to do in the new houses is to leave out the features that are shared, and to minimise living space. For example, because meals are available in the large communal kitchen every lunch and dinner time, and most people choose to make use of this offering, the need for large kitchens in each house is eliminated, as preparing meals becomes an occasional function rather than a daily routine. So the kitchens we have built are quite small. This saves considerably in construction costs, since the actual floor area is reduced and kitchens traditionally are expensive to build. But the houses still provide the privacy and necessary conveniences for living if the residents choose not to interact with the larger community.

In our first housing development, Bag End, we are building detached or semi-detached buildings and have included one communal building for larger gatherings, meetings, parties and occasional eating together. The other shared features include several small laundries, for two to four households; a common green and garden area; several rooms in one of the houses that are used for massage and holistic health treatments; some garden sheds with shared tools; a common heating system for several of the houses; a shared freezer: and eventually some storage and workshop space.

These are fairly minimal shared facilities, but there are others available on the site within short walking distance, including weaving and pottery studios; an art room; music practice rooms; a dance and exercise room; a volleyball court; and rooms large and small for meetings, parties and gatherings.

It is through a balanced degree of sharing that we can both save resources, energy and space and increase the quality of life and range of opportunities open to us.

Cost Considerations

Background

The most frequent questions we are asked about ecological houses are: 'How much do they cost?' and 'Do they cost more than "normal" houses?' The answer is that they need not cost more, as most of the products are inexpensive and fairly common. The layers are similar to those used in conventional construction, and most of the materials are relatively 'low-tech' with little processing involved in their production, which keeps costs minimal. The main component is softwood timber which need not be expensive if obtained locally (from sustainable sources of course!).

Where we have had to pay higher costs is in transportation. Some of the more ecologically advanced products are not made in the UK, like the Karlit medium board and the Celit 4-D profiled-edge bitumen board used as roof sarking. These we have had to import from Scandinavia and Germany, which has substantially increased their cost. For example, 4-D board is sold in Germany for £2.08/m². But the cost of transportation in the quantities we need increases that figure to £4.08/m², or nearly double. We have a similar problem with the special membranes that we use for roofing felt, breather paper and vapour check instead of plastic and ordinary felts and treated papers. These are produced in Germany and are more expensive to begin with, but the added cost of transport increases the square metre price even further.

One way that transportation costs could be reduced is through larger-scale importing and stocking in the UK. Some products we use that are made in Sweden — for example the Karlit medium board and SP windows — are available through distributors in Scotland and England. Because they are importing larger quantities, or even full containers or lorry loads, the relative increase in cost to us is minimal. Another advantage is that these products are more readily available if we need further supplies. As demand grows for the high quality, environmentally-friendly building materials that are now available on the continent, no doubt they will be imported and stocked here more widely.

Such products could also easily be manufactured in the UK if there were sufficient demand to justify the capital cost of facilities to produce them. But even with having to import a significant number of products from Europe there is no great difference in cost between our construction and so-called 'conventional' building. This will remain true of course only as long as transportation is cheap, due mainly to the artificially low price of oil. For the medium and long term it is to be hoped that the UK will have its own manufacturing base for these kinds of products.

Our Experience

Wall Construction: Comparing the costs of construction materials is relatively straightforward and the accompanying illustrations of wall construction show the make-up and cost per square metre of each element at February 1993 prices. The total cost of £19.78/m² for the breathing wall vs. £18.15/m² for a conventional timber frame construction represents a difference of 9%. An important consideration in comparing constructions is energy efficiency and the overall savings that will be made over the lifetime of the building by increased insulation (resulting in a lower thermal conductivity or 'U-value'). The breathing wall has a U-value of 0.19 W/m²°C compared to the conventional wall's U-value of 0.38 W/m²°C. In other words, for a 9% increase in construction cost you get a wall that loses 50% less energy. This relatively small difference in the initial cost will be recouped many times over in energy savings during the lifetime of the building.

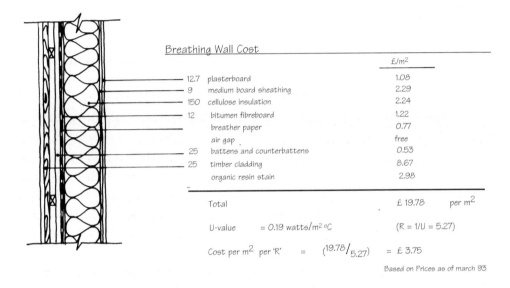

Breathing Wall Cost

		£/m²
12.7	plasterboard	1.08
9	medium board sheathing	2.29
150	cellulose insulation	2.24
12	bitumen fibreboard	1.22
	breather paper	0.77
	air gap	free
25	battens and counterbattens	0.53
25	timber cladding	8.67
	organic resin stain	2.98

Total   £ 19.78   per m²

U-value   = 0.19 watts/m² °C   (R = 1/U = 5.27)

Cost per m² per 'R'   =   ($^{19.78}/_{5.27}$)   = £ 3.75

Based on Prices as of march 93

Fig 5.18 Wall section costing: our construction

Another useful figure to look at is the cost per m² of construction vs. the thermal resistance of the wall. The thermal resistance (R), the inverse of the U-value, is simply the sum of the resistances the different elements of the wall offer to heat moving through it. In these terms the breathing wall at £3.75/m² per R is much more cost effective than the conventional wall at £6.90/m² per R. A lower cost per R means you get more for your money.

Roof Construction: A conventional type of layering costs £22.68/m², while the construction we are using is £29.14/m². This higher cost (28%) is due mainly to the use of clay tiles and the more expensive paper-based roofing felts. The clay tiles are made in France at £16.10/m² vs. concrete tiles at £11.10/m². We are currently investigating an English supplier of clay tiles that work out nearer the £11/m² mark. The special papers used for the vapour check (when medium board is not used), roofing felt and breather paper are hard to replace with any good environmental alternatives, but there are reinforced membranes available which are made from petrochemicals and the like. The most important physical characteristic to be checked in substitute membranes is permeability, remembering that the inside membrane needs to have some vapour resistance (but hopefully not too much if you are to maintain

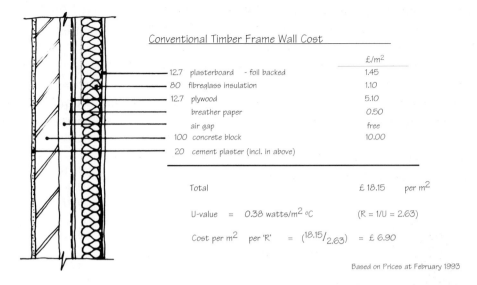

Conventional Timber Frame Wall Cost

		£/m²
12.7	plasterboard - foil backed	1.45
80	fibreglass insulation	1.10
12.7	plywood	5.10
	breather paper	0.50
	air gap	free
100	concrete block	10.00
20	cement plaster (incl. in above)	

Total		£ 18.15 per m²

U-value = 0.38 watts/m² °C   (R = 1/U = 2.63)

Cost per m² per 'R' = $(^{18.15}/_{2.63})$ = £ 6.90

Based on Prices at February 1993

Fig 5.19 Wall section costing: conventional construction

the 'breathing' characteristic) and the outside membranes need to have a low vapour resistance (i.e. be highly permeable). This is particularly important in the roof construction as conventional building felts, usually laid directly on the roof sarking (decking), are not permeable at all and would cause severe problems if used with our construction. It is essential either to provide a ventilated air space of at least 50 mm under a non-breathing roofing felt or to use a membrane that is vapour-permeable but moisture-proof (i.e. sheds water, such as 'Tyvec' roofing membranes).

Comparing the relative U-values for the two types of construction at 0.20 W/m²°C for our construction and 0.32 W/m²°C for the conventional construction, our roof loses 38% less heat for the 28% higher cost. Comparing the cost-per-m²-per-R value, as with the wall construction, the breathing roof is again more cost effective at £5.70/m² per R vs. £7.22/m² per R for a conventional wall.

There are sometimes big local variations in costs of various materials. For instance, if we were to use the English clay tiles instead of the more expensive French ones, our roof costs would come down to £24.37/m² — only 7.5% higher than normal. It pays to shop around and do your sums before committing yourself, as well as checking out the other criteria for ecological design mentioned previously.

It is a myth that 'ecological' building costs significantly more than conventional methods and we hope that these illustrations will help to dispel it.

The above discussion has dealt only with the material costs of building and not the related labour costs, which should also be mentioned.

The basic skills needed by any tradesperson for the kind of houses we are building here are not vastly different from normal. Most of the construction techniques are straightforward and can be carried out by anyone who has some aptitude for building. There are a few techniques, however, that are different and take some time to

Performance of Standard Roof vs Breathing Roof

mm	Material/Element	Thermal Conductivity (W/m°C)	Thickness (m)	Thermal Resistance (m²°C/W)	Cost per m² (£/m²)
Standard Roof Construction					
	Inside air film			0.100	
12.5	Plasterboard	0.160	0.013	0.078	1.45
100	Fibreglass	0.040	0.100	2.500	1.56
	Rafters 50x150 @ 600				1.87
50	Vented air space		0.050	0.180	
12.5	Plywood	0.144	0.013	0.087	5.10
	Roofing felt	0.500		0.011	0.65
	Counterbattens 25x38 @ 600				0.32
25	Vented air space		0.025	0.120	
	Tiling battens 25x38 @ 300				0.63
20	Concrete roof tiles	0.833	0.020	0.024	11.10
	Outside air film			0.040	

R =	**Thermal Resistance**	(m²°C/W)		**R = 3.14**	
U =	**Thermal Conductance**	(W/m²°C)		**U = 0.32**	

Total cost per square metre   £ 22.6?

Cost per square metre per R   £ 7.22

mm	Material/Element	(W/m°C)	(m)	(m²°C/W)	(£/m²)
Breathing Roof Construction					
	Inside air film			0.100	
12.5	Plasterboard	0.160	0.013	0.078	1.08
	Vapour check			0.011	0.87
150	Cellulose insulation	0.035	0.150	4.286	2.24
	Rafters 50x150 @ 600				1.63
22	Bitumen board	0.050	0.022	0.440	4.40
	Paper roofing membrane			0.011	1.65
	Counterbattens 50x50 @ 600				0.65
50	Vented air space		0.050	0.120	
	Tiling battens 25x38 @ 310				0.52
20	Clay pantiles	0.833	0.020	0.024	16.10
	Outside air film			0.040	

R =	**Thermal Resistance**	(m²°C/W)		**R = 5.11**	
U =	**Thermal Conductance**	(W/m²°C)		**U = 0.20**	

Total cost per square metre   £ 29.1?

Cost per square metre per R   £ 5.7?

Comparison   **£6.46/28.5% higher**

costs based on figures available Feb. 93

Fig 5.20

learn. Detailing for maximum energy efficiency, for instance, requires that a lot more care be taken in sealing window frames, fitting sheathing and overlapping and glue-ing air barriers like the exterior building paper. We ourselves have not always been successful at these things. Perhaps the most difficult process labour-wise has been the correct installation of the wet-blown insulation, which requires specialised equipment and operator skills. A builder used to getting rolls of fibreglass from his merchant and stuffing it casually into joist and stud spaces will probably regard the cellulose blowing machine, hoses, pumps and endless bags of insulation as a huge amount of extra work. When using this kind of system, it is generally better to employ a specialist rather than ask your own uninitiated builder to do it, unless you are prepared to hire equipment and have a go yourself.

5.30

What we have found from our experience is that the more skilled the builders are the easier and quicker the work goes. This may seem like a fairly obvious observation but often we have tended to have a higher proportion of unskilled to skilled workers. Over the years we have discovered that the proportion should be reversed for maximum efficiency and job enjoyment for all.

In general, after the initial learning of new techniques or skills, there need be no great difference in the time it takes to build ecological buildings compared with conventional ones and therefore there should be no great difference in labour costs.

Retrofitting Existing Buildings

Background

With the stabilisation of the population of most western countries the need for new housing has decreased since post-war days and will continue to decrease with the lower birth rate as baby boomers move through the housing market. There will always be the need for new housing, but there is a growing trend to upgrade the existing housing stock with major renovation work and increased energy efficiency using healthy and non-toxic materials.

It is quite relevant then to consider how we can incorporate green building principles into renovation work. In fact given the principles that have been discussed in this manual it is not at all difficult to apply them to work on older houses. All of the same criteria for choosing materials apply across the board, assessing their 'greenness' in terms of the environmental impact from extraction and manufacturing, energy consumption, transport, useful life, and health impact on installers and the eventual residents, as well as their ability to perform the function for which they were designed.

Fig 5.21
Cullerne House, built circa 1830

Because of the wide range of renovation work that is possible, from simple redecorating to major demolition and reconstruction, it is not possible to comment on all specific situations. But there are a few general areas for which some basic guidelines can be given.

An important consideration in a green renovation or retrofitting is the age of the building and what kind of materials were used and how 'healthy' they are. Most of the difficulties caused by outgassing will lessen with time, so in a 1950s' or 60s' building that may be full of chipboard and plastic it is reasonable to assume that most of the excess volatiles will have already passed out of the materials and they will be relatively stable. So as long as they are in good condition they need not be replaced. But if they do need replacing, then be sure not to use the same materials, as the problem will begin all over again.

Have your house tested for radon, especially if you have a basement. Small test kits at a nominal charge are available from Track Analysis Systems Limited (see Appendix E). Should you be above the recommended limit, then consult a specialist firm about taking specific measures to eliminate the problem.

Our Experience

The use of non-toxic natural materials for interior finishes need not be any different from that for new houses. Perhaps one of the most important areas is the choice of paints and finished wood treatments, since they will cover almost the entire inside surface area of the house and will have a great impact on the residents through their extensive exposure to these materials. We would strongly recommend the use of non-toxic organic paints and finishes for all aspects of redecorating since many of the alternatives do contain some of the more noxious compounds found in building products, from VOCs in paints and preservatives to formaldehyde in wallpaper

Fig 5.22
Renovation work

adhesives. We have found there is quite adequate choice of green decorating materials from the suppliers listed in the References and Sponsors sections. Depending on your location, it will probably require more planning time to use these products, as most paint supply stores will not carry them and they will need to be ordered in advance. It is worth writing direct to the manufacturers for their catalogue of products and applications, as well as for prices and distributors.

Another area that can easily be adapted to the green approach is that of sheet materials, plasterboard and the like. Using medium board and low-formaldehyde plywood (from sustainable sources of course) in place of chipboard, MDF and other plywoods is highly recommended, as these are some of the worst offenders in the battle against indoor air pollution.

In major renovation jobs, when walls are stripped back to studs, insulation is applied and rewiring done, all of the products and techniques we have discussed can normally be used — non-toxic materials to replace the fabric, wiring for minimal electrostress, an increase in insulation and energy efficiency, etc.

One very important point to emphasise in major renovation jobs, however, is the need to assess the wall, roof and floor construction carefully to determine what kind of vapour movement may occur. In most houses it is not appropriate to attempt to create a 'breathing wall' construction, as it is unlikely that the external skin of the building will have low enough permeability. It will almost certainly be necessary to incorporate some kind of vapour check or barrier on the inside surface. A green alternative to plastic or aluminium that is made from recycled paper and non-toxic glue is available from: Isofloc, Ökologische Bautechnik, Hirschhagen GmbH, Dieselstraße 3, 3436 Hessisch Lichtenau, Germany. Telephone 010-49-5602-80080.

We have a number of old properties that we maintain, generally 100-to-200-year-old stone buildings, and we have done extensive renovation on all of them. We have not always used the greenest of materials until recently, but have found that the transition is easy. The most difficult part has been the continual education of newer community members working in maintenance and renovations who do not realise that alternatives are available.

APPENDICES

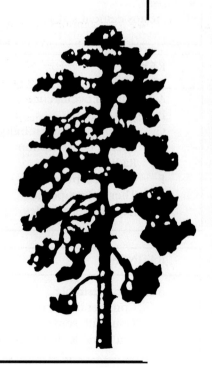

Material	A	B	C	D	E	F	G	H	I	K	L	M	N	O	P	Q	GRADE
1 Timber	3	3	3	3	3	3	3	3	3	3	3	3	3	3	3	3	3.0
2 Cork	3	3	3	3	3	3	3	3	3	3	3	3	3	3	3	3	3.0
3 Wood particle board	1	1	2	2	3	3	3	3		1	2	3	2	0	1		1.9
4 Hardboard	1	2	3	2	3	3	3	2		1	2	3	2	2	2		2.2
5 Veneered block board	2	2	3	2	3	3	3	3	3	1	2	3	2	1	2		2.3
6 Woodwool slab (magnesite bond)	2	2	3	2	3	3	3	3	3	3	3	3	3	3	2		2.7
7 Softboard	2	2	3	2	3	3	3	3	3	3	3	3	3	3	2		2.7
8 Coconut fibre products	3	2	3	2	3	3	3	3	3	3	3	3	3	3	3		2.9
9 Mineral fibres (from slag)	0	0	0	0	0	2	3	3		0	0	3		0			0.9
10 Glass fibre (syn. resin bonded)	0	0	0	0	3	1	3	3		0	0	3		0	0	0	0.9
11 Polystyrene	0	0	0	0	3	0	3	3	0	1	0	3	0	0	0	0	0.8
12 PVC products (hard)	0	0	0	0	3	0	1	2	0	0	0	3	0	0	0		0.6
13 Synthetic resin glue	0	0	0	0	3	0				0	0	3	0	0	0		0.5
14 Synthetic resin varnish	0	0	0	0	3	0				0	0			0	0	0	0.3
15 Synthetic woodstains	0	0	0	1	3	3				3	3			0	0		1.3
16 Beeswax & products	3	3	3	3	3	3				3	3		3	3	3		3.0
17 Asphalt & bitumen felts & paper	1	0	1	1	3	3				0	0	0		0	0		0.8
18 Vapour barrier (foil)	0	0	0	0	3	0				0	0	0		0	0	0	0.3
19 Brick products	2	3	3	2	2	3	2	3	3	2	1	3	2	3	3		2.5
20 Clay	3	3	3	3	3	3	3	3	3	3	3	2	3	3	3		2.9
21 Ceramic products (unglazed)	2	2	2	2	2	3	1	2		1	0	3		3	3		2.0
22 Concrete (reinforced w/ steel)	0	0	0	0	1	1	0	1	0	0	0	0	0	3	0	0	0.4
23 Pumice blocks	1	0	1	2	0	2	2	2		2	1	0		3	0	0	1.1
24 Synthetic gypsum	0	0	0	1	0		1	2	0	2	2	3		3	1	0	1.1
25 Cement mortar (cement fr. slag)	1	0	2	1	0	3	1	2		1	2	0	1	3	1		1.3
26 Lime mortar	2	2	3	2	3	3	1	2		2	3	2	2	3	2		2.3
27 Limestone	1	2	3	2	2	3	2	2		1	2	1		3	2		2.0
28 Synthetic resin plaster	0	0	0	1		0	1	2		0	0	3	0	0	0		0.5
29 Linoleum	1	2	3	2	3	3	2	2	3	2	2	3	3	3	3		2.5
30 Glass	0	1	1	0	3	0	0	0		0	0	3	0	3	3		1.0
31 Asbestos cement slabs	1	0	0	1	1		2	2	0	1	2	3		3	1	0	1.2

KEY	
A Natural occurrence	I Resistance to microwaves
B Test of time	K Diffusion/breathing properties
C Ecological compatibility	L Hygroscopicity
D Energy consumption	M Moisture content/drying time
E Radioactivity	N Absorption, regeneration
F Electrical properties	O Toxic vapours and gases
G Thermal properties	P Smell
H Acoustic properties	Q Skin resistance

RATINGS

3 Very desirable
2 Commendable, only minor shortcomings
1 Doubtful, some shortcomings
0 Undesirable due to considerable shortcomings

Source:
Working Papers in Building Biology, Chapter 8, Part II

A. Ecological Assesment of Building Materials
see previous page

B. Energy Requirement for Manufacturing and/or Producing Selected Building Materials

	Material	kWh/tonne	kWh/m³
1	Fletton bricks	175	300
2	Non-fletton bricks	860	1,462
3	Engineering bricks	1,120	2,016
4	Clay tiles	800	1,520
5	Concrete tiles	300	630
6	Local stone tiles	200	450
7	Local slates	200	540
8	Single layer roof membrane	45,000	47,000
9	Concrete 1:3:6	275	600
10	Concrete 1:2:4	360	800
11	Lightweight blocks	500	600
12	Autoclaved blocks	1,300	800
13	Natural sand/aggregate	30	45
14	Crushed granite aggregate	100	150
15	Lightweight aggregate	500	300
16	Cement	2,200	2,860
17	Sand/cement render	277	400
18	Plaster/plasterboard	890	900
19	Steel	13,200	103,000
20	Copper	15,000	133,000
21	Aluminium	27,000	75,600
22	Timber (imported softwood)	1,450	7,540
23	Timber (local airdried)	200	110
24	Timber (local green oak)	200	220
25	Glass	9,200	23,000
26	Plastics	45,000	47,000
27	Plastic insulation		1,125
28	Mineral wool		230
29	Cellulose insulation		133
30	Woodwool (loose)		900

Source: Pat Borer, Centre for Alternative Technology

Note: The exact energy needed to produce building products & materials is very difficult to determine and the above figures should be taken as a rough guide only.

Product	Insulation Type	Price per Unit	Unit	k-Value	R-Value @150mm	U-Value @150mm	Cellulose Equivalent @150mm	Cost per R per m²	Cost/m² Cellu. equiv. @150mm
Warm Cell	cellulose 50 kg/m³	£ 5.20	17.5 Kg	0.035	4.29	0.233	150	£ 0.52	£ 2.23
Isofloc	cellulose 45 kg/m³	£ 6.10	15.0 Kg	0.035	4.29	0.233	150	£ 0.64	£ 2.75
Superglass	glass fibre	£ 2.40	m² @ 150mm	0.040	3.75	0.267	172	£ 0.64	£ 2.75
Rockwool	mineral fibre	£ 2.34	m² @ 150mm	0.037	4.05	0.247	159	£ 0.58	£ 2.48
K-Cell	expanded polystyrene	£ 6.37	1220x2440 50mm sheet	0.037	4.05	0.247	159	£ 1.58	£ 6.79
Polyfoam Plus	extruded polystyrene	£ 6.40	m² @ 50mm	0.027	5.56	0.180	116	£ 3.46	£ 14.83
Shelterfoil B9 CFC free	polyurethane foam board	£ 5.32	m² @ 35mm	0.023	6.52	0.153	99	£ 3.50	£ 15.00
Shelterfoil CFC blown	polyurethane foam board	£ 4.20	m² @ 35mm	0.022	6.82	0.147	94	£ 2.64	£ 11.33

k-Value	Thermal Conductivity	watts/m°C	Inherent insulation property of a material. Lower value means it is a better insulator.
R-Value	Thermal Resistance	m²°C/watt	R=thickness in metres/k. It means resistance to heat loss. Higher is better.
U-Value	Thermal Conductance	watts/m²°C	U=1/R The common measure for heat loss in Britain. Lower is better.

Prices shown are trade prices as of July 1992.

Insulation values and price comparison.

C. Comparison of Common Insulation Materials.

see previous page

D. Sponsors and Suppliers List

Name	Address & Telephone	Products
Aberdeen Windows & Doors Systems Ltd.	83-87 Causewayend Aberdeen AB2 3TQ Scotland, UK 01224 633 174	Swedoor & Hovland External Doors - high quality, energy-efficient
AES, Ltd.	Appropriate Energy Systems The Park, Forres, Moray, IV36 0TZ Scotland, UK 01309 690 132	Makers of solar flat plate collector & systems. "Weatherwise Double Sun"
AF/Armaflex	Armstrong House 38 Market Square Uxbridge UB8 1NG England, UK 01895 251 122	Non-CFC (ozone-friendly) pipe insulation
Airflow Developments Ltd.	Cressex Ind'l Estate Lancaster Road High Wycombe HP12 3QP England, UK 01494 25252	Extractor fans
Auro Organic	Unit 1, Goldstones Farm Ashdon Saffron Walden CB10 2LZ England, UK 01799 584 888	Organic paints & non-toxic wood preservatives
Armitage Shanks	Armitage Rugeley Staffordshire WS15 4BT England, UK 01543 490 253	Sanitaryware

Benson Environmental	Queens House Holly Road Twickenham TW1 4EG England, UK 0181 783 0033	Convector Radiators Underfloor heating Trench & Duct heating Kampmann Products
Biologische Insel	Rheintalsraße 35-43 6830 Schwetzingen- -Hirschacker Germany (+49) 6202 3016	Reinforced paper roofing felts and vapour checks
Conex Sanbra	Whitehall Road Great Bridge, Tipton West Midlands DY4 7JU England, UK 0121 557 2831	Copper plumbing fittings
Crosslee Trisave	Aberpark Ind'l Estate Aber Road, Flint Clwyd CH6 5EX Wales, UK 01352 762 061	Gas condensing boilers
Crucial Trading Ltd	The Market hall Craven Arms Shropshire SY7 9NY England, UK 01588 673666	Natural floor coverings coir, sisal, seagrass
Dunstable Rubber Co.	Eastern Avenue Luton Road, Dunstable Bedfordshire, LU5 4JY England, UK 01582 607 718	Hypalon' synthetic rubber membranes for turf roofs and geotextile mats
Euro Scandinavian	Southern House Station Approach Edenbridge Kent TN8 5LP England, UK 01732 867 868	'Karlit' medium board structural sheathing board , it's brilliant. and other fibre boards.

	Karlit AB S-810 64 Karlsholmsbruk Sweden +46 (0) 294 406 40	Swedish parent company for 'Karlit' sheathing
Excel Industries Ltd	13 Rassau Ind'l Estate Ebbw Vale Gwent NP3 5SD Wales, UK 01495 350 655	Cellulose insulation. 'Warmcel Light' with training programme available
Expamet Building Products	PO Box 52 Longhill Industrial Estate Hartlepool Cleveland TS25 1PR England, UK 01429 866 611	Metal fixings
Fels-Werke GmbH	P.O. Box 1460 D-38640 Goslar 1 Germany +49 (0) 5321 70330	'Fermacell' rigid gypsum board. (Made in Germany)
	8 Trinity Place Midland Drive Sutton Coldfield B72 1TX England, UK 0121 321 1155	UK sales
Forbo-Nairn Ltd	PO Box 1 Kirkcaldy, Fife, KY1 2SB Scotland, UK 01592 643 111	Manufacturers of natural linoleum
Ifö Sanitar AB	Box 140 S-29500 Bromölla Sweden +46 (0) 456 280 00	Water conserving toilets. 3.5 litre flush, the lowest available. (Made in Sweden)

Isofloc	Okologische Bautechnik Hirschhagen GmbH Dieselstraße 3 3436 Hessisch Lichtenau +49 (0) 5602-80080	Cellulose Insulation Building Biology approved products.
Isofloc UK	31 Heathfield Stacey Bushes Milton Keynes MK12 6HR 01908-314485	Cellulose insulation Distributor for many other green products.
Josiah Parkes & Sons Ltd	Union Works, Gower Street, Willenhall West Midlands WV13 1JX England, UK 01902 366 931	Lock sets
Klober Ltd	Pear Tree Words Upper Langford Avon BS18 7DJ England, UK 01934 853 224	'Tyvek' building paper suppliers.
Lucas Rists Wiring Systems	Cable Division, Lower Mile House Lane Newcastle-under-Lyme Staffordshire ST5 9BT England, UK 01782 562 988	Electric cable
Meynell Valves Ltd.	Shaw Road Bushbury Wolverhampton WV10 9LB England, UK 01902 28621	Mixer taps
MK Electrics Ltd.	The Arnold Centre Paycock Road Basilton, Essex SS14 3EA England, UK 0181 803 3355	Electrical accessories and fittings

Natural Therapeutics	25 New Road Spalding Lincolnshire PE11 1DJ England, UK 01775 761 927	Demand switch circuit breakers for reducing EMFs & electrical field stress
Naylor Brothers (Clayware) Ltd	Clough Green Cawthorne Green Barnsley S75 4AD South Yorkshire England, UK 01226 790 591	Clay drainage pipe
Osram GEC.	PO Box 17, East Lane Wembley, Middlesex HA9 7PG England, UK 0811 904 4321	Low energy light bulbs (compact fluorescent)
Redland Plasterboard	Redland House Reigate, Surrey RH2 0SJ England, UK 01737 242 488	Plasterboard
Robert Bosch Ltd.	PO Box 98 Broadwater Park North Orbital Road Denham Uxbridge UB9 5HJ England, UK 01895 834 466	Power tools
Rockwool Ltd.	Pencoed, Bridgend Mid Glamorgan CF35 6NY Wales, UK 01656 862 621	Insulation materials

Rothenberger (UK) Ltd.	14-18 Tenter Road, Moulton Park Industrial Estate, Northampton NN3 1PS England, UK 01604 646 231	Plumbing tools
Sandvik Saws & Tools UK	Manor Way, Halesowen, West Midlands B62 8QZ England, UK 0121 550 4700	Hand tools
Senco Fasteners (UK) Ltd.	211 Europa Boulevard Gemini Business Park West Brook, Warrington Cheshire WA5 5TN England, UK 01925 445 566	Pneumatic nail guns
Snickers Original	Snickers Centre 1275 Stratford Road Hall Green, Birmingham B28 8BR England, UK 0121 778 5041	Tool jackets & work clothes. Made in Sweden, sold widely in Europe.
Somerville Nails Ltd.	Station Road Lennox Town Nr. Glasgow G65 7JL Scotland, UK 01360 311 347	Nails
SP Snickerier AB (Windows & Doors)	P.O. Box 23217, Sveavagen 163 S-104 35 Stockholm Sweden +46 (0)8 34 69 46	Triple glazed windows & doors made in Sweden. Largest manufacturer in Europe

Stora/SP Windows	ESPE House Barton Turn, Barton under Needwood Staffs DE13 8EB 01283 716 660	UK Distributor for SP Windows
Stadium Building Products	Building Products Div. Unit 10, Morson Road, London EN3 4TU England, UK 0181 804 4343	Hard hats
T & D Ltd.	Bowling House Bowling Iron Works Bradford West Yorkshire BD4 8SR England, UK 01274 728 285	Water tanks and jackets
Tarkett Ltd.	Poyle House, P.O. Box 173, Colnbrook Slough, Berks. SL3 0AZ, England, UK 01753 684 533	Hardwood flooring. Made in Sweden
Tilcon Scotland Ltd.	250 Alexandra Parade Glasgow G31 3AX Scotland, UK 0141 554 1818	Ready mixed concrete
The Velux Company Ltd.	Telford Road Glenrothes East Fife KY7 4 NX Scotland, UK 01592 772 211	Roof lights and accessories
Vestas-Danish Wind Technologies A/S	Smed Hansens VEJ 27 DK 6940 LEM +45 (0) 97 341 188	Wind turbines from 75kW to 650kW capacity.

Watco (Sales) Ltd	Watco House Filmer Grove Godalming Surrey GU7 3AL England, UK 01483 425 000	Timberex' non-toxic wood floor treatment
Wednesbury Tube	Oxford Street Bilston West Midlands WV14 7DS England, UK 01902 491 133	Copper pipe

E.   References and Book List

Books

Alaska Craftsman Home Building Manual: A Guide for Energy Efficient Home Building in Alaska, Alaska Craftsman Home Program Inc., Richard D. Seifert, editor. University of Alaska, 1991. A thorough and exceptional manual for energy-efficient timber construction methods. It does cover health aspects of building materials.

Canadian Wood-Frame House Construction, Canada Mortgage & Housing Corporation (CMHC). Second metric edition, 1988. A good general guide to timber construction and detailing. CMHC also offers a large range of pamphlets covering everything from radon to moisture control, with emphasis on energy efficiency.

The Healthy Home, Linda Mason Hunter. Pocket Books, 1990.

Indoor Pollution, Steve Coffel and Karyn Feiden. Ballantine Books, 1991.

The Nontoxic Home, Debra Lynn Dadd. St Martin's Press, 1986.

The Natural House Book, David Pearson. Gaia Books, 1989. Excellent primer for all aspects of design of the healthy house, with background on materials, design principles and systems; beautifully illustrated with drawings and colour photographs.

Working Papers in Building Biology, Institute of Building Biology, c/o Hartwin Busch, Tara Cottage, Rectory Lane, Ashdon, Saffron Walden, Essex, CB10 2ET. Awkward translation of the German system of Baubiologie, it covers the theory and basic concepts and philosophy but often lacks the detail to translate into workable practice. A good reference.

Floors and Flooring, Jane Lott. Conran Octopus, 1985. Covers wide range of conventional and natural floor coverings. Basic guide.

Fragile Majesty, Keith Ervin. The Mountaineers, 1989. Tells the story of the ancient forests of Northwest America and their fate at the hands of timber interests.

Clinical Ecology, Dr George Lewith and Dr Julian Kenyon. Thorsons, 1985.

The English Country Cottage, R. J. Brown. Hamlyn Paperbacks, 1979. Historical look at the architectural development of the English cottage. Well illustrated with line drawings.

Gentle Architecture, Malcolm Wells. McGraw-Hill,1981. One of the first books on underground or earth-sheltered buildings. By the foremost architect in the field.

Hazardous Building Materials: A Guide to the Selection of Alternatives, Ed. S. R. Curwell & C. G. March. E. & F.N. Spon, 1986. Conventional look at modern materials and substances from a strictly scientific approach. Interesting as a reference to balance the 'all green' approach.

Building Technology, Ivor H. Seeley. The MacMillan Press, 1980. A basic book on conventional building detailing and techniques. Handy to have around, for everything from foundations to roofs.

The New Solar Home Book, Bruce Anderson. Brick House, 1987. Good reference on solar energy, both active and passive. Weather data for America only.

The Good Wood Guide, Simon Counsell. Friends of the Earth, 1990.

Greener Building: Products and Services Directory, Keith Hall and Peter Warm. Association of Environment Conscious Building, 1992. A new directory with good background information on natural resources, energy and industrial processes as well as products and suppliers of ecological materials.

The Timber-Frame Home, Tedd Benson. The Taunton Press, 1988. A wonderful book on the fine art of traditional post and beam construction. Beautifully illustrated.

Building the Timber Frame House, Tedd Benson with James Gruber. Charles Scribners Sons, 1980. More detailed look at the 'how to's of post and beam construction. Excellent reference for traditional joints and overall design.

Pollution Reduction Through Energy Conservation: A Report Prepared for Eurisol UK Ltd, J. R. Bowdidge, Eurisol UK Ltd, 39 High Street, Reboum, Herts AL3 7LW. Facts and figures on energy savings from insulation. Very useful for comparative levels and pollution savings.

From Eco-Cities to Living machines, Principles of Ecological Design, Nancy Jack Todd & John Todd, North Atlantic Books, 1994. Excellent reference for all aspects of ecological design, especially for waste water treatment and agriculture.

The Straw Bale House, Athena Swntzell Steen, Bill Steen, David Bainbridge, chelsea Green Publishing Company, 1994. The premier book on what is to be one of the new forms of eco-building in the future.

Building With Heart, A Practical Approach to Self and Community Building, Christopher Day, Green Books, 1990. Great philolsophy and case studies in community building and buildings.

The Permaculture Way, Priactical steps to create a self-sustaining world, Graham Bell, Thorsons (Harper Collins), 1992. Great introduction to Permaculture for northern latititudes.

Earth to Spirit, In Search of Natural Architecture, David Pearson, Gaia Books, 1994. Another must book for anyone interested in beautiful, natural built forms. Great images and photos.

Magazines and Articles

Fine Home Building, 63 South Main Street, PO Box 5506, Newtown, CT 06470-0933, USA. A must for builders — premier American magazine on building, with excellent illustrations and photographs. Of particular interest: Issue No. 73 Spring 1992, article by Kevin Ireton: 'An Environmental Showcase', on nontoxic materials.

Caduceus, Holistic Medicine, Natural Science & Creative Learning, 38j Russell Terrace, Leamington Spa, Warwickshire CV31 1HE, England. Particularly Issue No. 7, Summer 1989 on sick buildings or healing houses.

EcoDesign, Journal of the Ecological Design Association, 20 High Street, Stroud, Gloucestershire GL5 1AS, England. New UK publication with good articles on all relevant aspects of ecological building and design.

Scottish Wildlife, Magazine of the Scottish Wildlife Trust, No. 14, Autumn 1991. Article on timber management.

In Context, A Quarterly of Humane Sustainable Culture, Context Institute, PO Box 11470, Bainbridge Island, WA 98110, USA. Excellent coverage of wide range of subjects related to sustainable living, from social, cultural and human potential issues to building and eco-villages.

Permaculture Magazine, Solutions for Sustainable Living, Permanent Publications, Hyden House Ltd., Little Hyden Lane, Clanfield, Hampshire, PO8 0RU, England. Great UK publication based on principles of Permaculture, with many articles and ideas for gardening and living sustainably.

Clean Slate, The Journal of the Alternative Technology Association, Centre for Alternative Technology Publications, Machynlleth, Powys SY20 9AZ. Excellent source for everything needed for living in the 21st Century.

OneEarth, quarterly, from the Findhorn Foundation Community, OneEarth Ltd., The Park, Findhorn, Forres, IV36 0TZ.

Organisations

Association for Environment Conscious Building, Windlake House, The Pump Field, Coaley, Gloucestershire GL1 5DX, England Tel. (01453) 890757 Fax (01453) 834060.

British Earth Sheltering Association, c/o Peter Carpenter, Caer Llan Berm House, Lydart, Monmouth, Gwent NP5 4JJ, Wales. Tel. (01600) 860359.

Centre for Alternative Technology, The Quarry, Machynlleth, Powys SY20 9AZ, Wales. Tel. (01654) 702400.

Constructive Individuals, 36 Scarcroft Road, York YO2 1NF, England. Tel. (01904) 625300. Fax (01904) 625301.

Eco-Arc, Ecological Architectural Practice, c/o Andrew Yeats, Cottage Studios, Red House Farm, Flaxton, York YO6 7SH, England. Tel. (01904) 86752.

Ecological Design Association, 20 High Street, Stroud, Gloucestershire GL5 1AS, England. Tel. (01453) 765575.

Findhorn Foundation Development, Planning Office, The Park, Findhorn, Morayshire IV36 0TZ, Scotland. Tel. (01309) 690154. Fax (01309) 691387.

Institute of Building Biology, c/o Hartwin Busch, Tara Cottage, Rectory Lane, Ashdon, Saffron Walden, Essex CB10 2ET, England. Tel. (01799) 584727.

Ökologische Bautechnik, Hirschhagen GmbH, Dieselstraße 3, 3436 Hessisch Lichtenau, Germany, Telephone +49 (0) 5602-80080.

Radon Testing Service, Track Analysis Systems Limited, H.H. Wills Physics Laboratory, Tyndall Avenue, Bristol BS8 1TL, England.

Timber Research and Development Association (TRADA), Stocking Lane, Hughenden Valley, High Wycombe, Bucks. HP14 4ND, England. Tel. (01494) 563091. Fax (01494) 565487.

F.   Eco-Villages and Sustainable Communities

In 1982 the Findhorn Foundation hosted a conference called "Building a Planetary Village" which was attended by some 250 participants from around the world. The theme of the conference was the development of a sustainable model of human living: a 'planetary' (or ecological) village that incorporates our need for environmental harmony as well as addresses the needs for a deeper, more fulfilling and connected existence to the rest of life on the planet.

It was clear then, as it is even more so now, that the environmental problems facing the human race, as well as threatening the planet, are the result of our limited understanding or consciousness of the world and how it works. It is the thinking behind our actions which is the real problem and only by addressing and correcting our collective thinking will the problems be dealt with at a causal level. It requires of us a change of consciousness, an expansion of how we have perceived life and the world up till now.

Essentially it is that we humans are not the centre of the Universe, only a part of it. We are one species within a complex web of life with millions of species: from the single cell organisms of our first ancestors three and a half billion years ago to the giant blue whale of today, the largest animal that has ever lived on this planet. These species and every one in between are what makes up life on Earth; each has a niche to fill, a part to play.

Somewhere along the line of our evolution we have lost sitght of this larger context of life, forgotten our part, lost our way. It is only because of this that we continue to make choices which cause the destruction of life rather than act to protect and enhance it. We as a race simply cannot exist in isolation, without the life-support systems regulated by the complex collective action of the life-forms within the biosphere, so beautifully described in *Gaia, a New Look at Life on Earth* by James Lovelock. We are a part of a living planet.

Only by rediscovering this truth can we begin to make our choices and shape our physical habitat to coexist with, rather than destroy, our environment. Technical solutions to these very real problems, from ozone depletion due to CFC's to indoor pollution from formaldehyde, be they environmentally friendly or not, are not lasting solutions unless they reflect and consider this larger context of life.

It was from this conference in 1982 that the Foundation was seeded in its work with the built environment. The concept of eco-villages, a universally applicable, sustainable model for human living that attempts to embody the "think globally and act locally" axiom, is one that does try to embrace the larger context of life. If we humans are to find our place again, to know what our part is, then we must also have the things around us that nurture us as human beings, that help us to grow, to deepen our understanding through education and experience, and to become more whole in ourselves.

True sustainability then cannot simply be about eco-gadgets, insulation, solar panels and organic paints — the things that this book talks about. To create a true human ecology our communities must also include aspects of sustainability in our social and cultural structures; in our economic systems of trade, manufacturing and services; and in what we call the spiritual dimension or 'larger context' of life, which is simply about our connection to the rest of creation. These elements of sustainability combined with ecological and environmental aspects are fundamental to an eco-village: an environment where human beings can fully grow and mature with wisdom, compassion and understanding.

Eco-Villages can be built anywhere on the planet: in an isolated area or in the middle of a teeming city. The location is not important because the principles can be applied whatever the conditions. It is this consciousness of cooperation, of interdependence, of respect for life and our human part within it which is the keynote and what will hold it together. The physical form or expression of these villages can and will adapt to reflect the local conditions and needs. They will be unique and organic expressions of the people and place of which they are a part.

We hope that the accompanying diagram is of help in understanding this concept. Without this larger context it would seem that ecological methods of building are of no consequence and cannot make a difference in the long run. It is our wish that the inspiration and hope for a positive future that we have felt in working with this concept and the resulting project here at the Findhorn Foundation will also touch and inspire others.

FINDHORN FOUNDATION

Towards a Planetary Village

...what is it all about...

A human ecology that is sustainable spiritually, culturally, economically and ecologically; that expresses our own essential relation and connectedness to spirit and nature through its forms and structures.

planetary

Planetary becomes - to highlight an awareness and participation in the evolutionary expansion of consciousness through-out the planetary system. An awareness that humanity is not separate from the rest of nature, but life is interdependent and interconnected with all life on our planet-Gaia.

village

Village becomes - to mark our transition from an extended family / community to a diverse and interactive village organisation. As with a traditional village we are developing a greater domestic base, greater interaction with the local area and more reliance on the land that supports our very existence.

Spiritually Sustainable

Our relationship to the larger context of life and the Greater Reality of which we are a part: i. The spiritual dimension of our own divinity. ii. Gaia and the planetary system. iii. Our greater purpose for being here now. iv. and our real connectedness to all life.

Process of spiritual growth.

- **Truth** – clear reflection of real truth by experience
- **Expansion** – awareness grows with expansion of consciousness
- **Love & Peace** – embracing of the individual
- **Transformation** – realignment within the individual

The inner foundation and purpose of the village is based on the spiritual invocation that God is accessible. Native to alive, and the environment is supportive of transformation.

Economically Sustainable

Small scale business, crafts and services that create maximum diversity of economic base and a rich ecology of financial income and job opportunities.

- Cottage Industries & crafts
- Co-operatives
- Shops
- Consulting
- Manufacturing
- Education
- Local Services
- Trading
- Printing Publishing

Maximum recycling of cash with-in the village before import and export.
Import ← (cash & products) — (cash & products) → Export

Ecologically Sustainable

Sustainable physical systems and structures that are integrated into the existing natural environment around us. Each micro-cosm or system self sustaining within its self but interdependent and inter-connected with larger macro-cosm of the whole.

- **Energy** – min. consumption, max renewables: 70% wind, 20% solar, 10% wood, 0% fossil.
- **Waste** – 100% composting of organics recycling sewage water. Paper metal, glass, super safe sanitisation of burnables.
- **Food** – soil produced in-house organic-seasonal eating balanced with green house production.
- **Housing** – construction with land - high insulation, low energy common land - use diverse terrain.

Culturally Sustainable

Satisfying our need as human beings to be creative and expressive; to learn, grow, teach and be; to have a diverse, intercultural, stimulating and exciting social environment and range of experiences available.

- Performing Arts
- Cultural Events
- Job Diversity
- Creative Arts
- Social Diversity
- Personal Growth
- Health Wholeness
- Physical Rec.
- Skill Development

The cycle and diversity of cultural and creative experiences nurtures us as human beings.

Existing Site Plan

- Pineridge
- Sand Dunes
- The Park
- Cullerne Gardens
- Findhorn Bay

North

G   Strawbale construction

Background

Straw, reeds and grasses have been recognised as valuable building materials for thousands of years by traditional cultures throughout the world. particularly in regions where timber and stone are scarce (e.g. around major river deltas).

With the development of modern baling equipment in the late 1800s, compressed and baled meadow hay began to be used like large building bricks. This first occurred in America and the inspiration seems to have come only partly from a lack of locally available building materials. What has come to be known as the Nebraska style house (a load-bearing bale structure) seems to have initially been envisaged as temporary shelter until enough money had been saved to build a 'real house'. Ultimately these temporary structures were accepted as 'real houses' at which point external walls, previously left exposed, were finished with a thick coat of mud plaster or cement render.

Post and beam structures, with strawbale used as a non-load-bearing infill, were being built in the Great Plains in the early 1940s. But a short time later strawbale construction virtually stopped, most likely because of the dramatic increase in the availability of cheap mass-produced materials after the war.

The 1980s marked an enthusiastic revival in the use of strawbale. Examples from North America in the early 1900s as well as those in more recent years from the USA, Canada, France, Finland and Mexico, show the very great potential of this material for ecological construction.

The benefits of strawbale are many and totally in keeping with ecological building standards. Straw is biodegradable, grows in a short period of time and in some regions of the world is considered a waste product and still burned off. The nature of straw means it can be used to create "breathing" structures. Insulation values are generally two to three times better than most well-insulated houses. Also the relatively easy construction of strawbale structures is perfect for self-building projects.

Our Experience — Strawbale Shed

We wanted to experiment with strawbale and so chose to do a small tool shed (8.2 x 4.4 m) as a demonstration project for the Eco-Villages & Sustainable Communities Conference held at the Foundation in 1995. The workshop was led by David Eisenberg from Tucson, Arizona, an expert in strawbale and one of the contributing authors to The Strawbale Book, the current bible on the subject.

Given the limited size of the building, its uncomplicated design, short roof span and lightweight roof structure, we opted for load-bearing bale walls. Bale quality and density are especially important in load-bearing structures, as the bales, unlike conventional building materials, are compressible. In a structure with standard loads and well-compacted bales, the settlement should be relatively small and occur during the first two to three months.

Barley straw is prevalent locally, though the vast majority is now baled in large cylindrical bales to reduce labour costs. However, we did find a source nearby where the farmer was willing to bale the straw to our specification. Ultimately we lost this initial source, as the farmer's harvest was ruined during an untimely week of non-stop rain. We did find another source, but we were not able to get the bale density we wanted. This led later to quite a lot of settlement and to the conclusion that forward planning is essential to assure a supply of quality bales.

Prior to the workshop, bales were stacked nearby, covered with polyethylene tarpaulins. Wet bales where moisture content rises above about 20% can get fungal growth inside the bale before drying is possible. Not what you want in your finished walls, so keep your bales dry!

During the three afternoons when the workshop was run, all of the bale walls were built except the upper sections of the gable ends. Supervision is vital during the bale-raising phase of the project; great enthusiasm can result in considerably out-of-plumb walls on which extra time will inevitably need to be spent during the finishing of the building. We had plenty of experience of this!

There need be very little waste in a strawbale construction, as loose straw and cut ties can all be reused to fill gaps and help even out surfaces. We used a plywood box beam as a bearing plate on top of the walls to distribute the loads from the rafters. The box bean also adds stability to the walls and provides a tie down for the roof to the foundation. Tie downs were simple turn buckles and steel wire, at 1.2 metre centres. The box beam also served as a compression beam for pre-stressing the walls, something which helps ensure that settlement from live loads does not continue to occur over a longer period.

Much deliberation was put into the specification of wall finishes. For the most part the options all involved maintaining a 'breathing' wall construction and initially focused on the possibility of using a traditional lime render.

Experiments with earth render for the internal walls involved the use of sieved soil with a clay content of less than 30%, chopped straw and water. Two coats were applied, both with the hands, the initial coat with fingers forcing the earth render mixture in between the strands of straw in order to create a good key. This resulted in a layer which was 'pitted' and hence provided, in turn, a key for the next coat which was smoothed over to create a gently undulating surface.

The final application to the internal walls differed only in the addition of a commercial mortar plasticiser, builders lime (dry hydrated lime) and sand. The plasticiser was added as a binder, the sand to balance a higher percentage of clay and the builders lime to increase hardness of the surface. The first coat was predominantly applied by hand and left to go off for a few hours after which damp foam rubber was used to smooth the surface. The application of a top coat was carried out with a float trowel, and included more finely chopped straw than the first coat. It was found that, by reducing the time between the application of the coats, a better bond was established, as the base coat tends to pull moisture out of the top coat if it has been allowed to dry more. Shrinkage cracks mostly appeared after two to three days; however these were easily filled and smoothed out in the top coat.

Largely for reasons of cost, an earth render of slightly different composition to that of the internal walls was opted for rather than a traditional lime-render finish. As a result of finding that certain areas internally were somewhat vulnerable to impact, the quantity of hydrated lime in the external mix was increased. Either a commercial waterproof/plasticiser or emulsified bitumen (apparently the latter has been used successfully as waterproofing for adobe finish in British Columbia) was added to the mix and applied to different walls.

Basic proportions were: 12 shovels of earth, 3 shovels of dry hydrated lime, 2 shovels of sand, and water to consistency. Chopped straw was added to the base coat only, in order to avoid the exposure of small pieces of straw on the outer most surface. The base coat was applied so as to build out hollows and areas of less well compacted straw. Chicken-wire was also used in those areas of the wall where the straw was particularly loose; this was pushed into the base coat a few hours after its application with the use of metal ties. As with the internal walls, less shrinkage occurred when the top coat was applied soon after the the base coat, rather than allowing the base to dry out too much. Hairline cracks were much slower to appear on the external wall surfaces than on internal walls, often occurring as much as two to three weeks after application.

The strawbale structure has a simple beauty and accessibility. Straw is a natural and readily available material; the insulation values are significantly better than average construction; a wide range of wall finishes allows the structures to breathe. It can be easily erected by a group of unskilled people for whom it will be fun and an empowering experience!

Appendix G was written by Nicole Edmonds and John Talbott © 1997